SHIRIN AZARI

STORIES OF LITTLE AND BIG BLOSSOMS

Elham und die neue Schule

Elham and Her New School

Elham und ihre Familie sind einmal mehr in
eine neue Stadt gezogen. Seit sie aus dem Iran
fliehen mussten, haben sie schon an vielen
verschiedenen Orten gelebt.

Elham and her family have moved yet again
to a new city. Since they had to flee Iran, they've
lived in lots of different places.

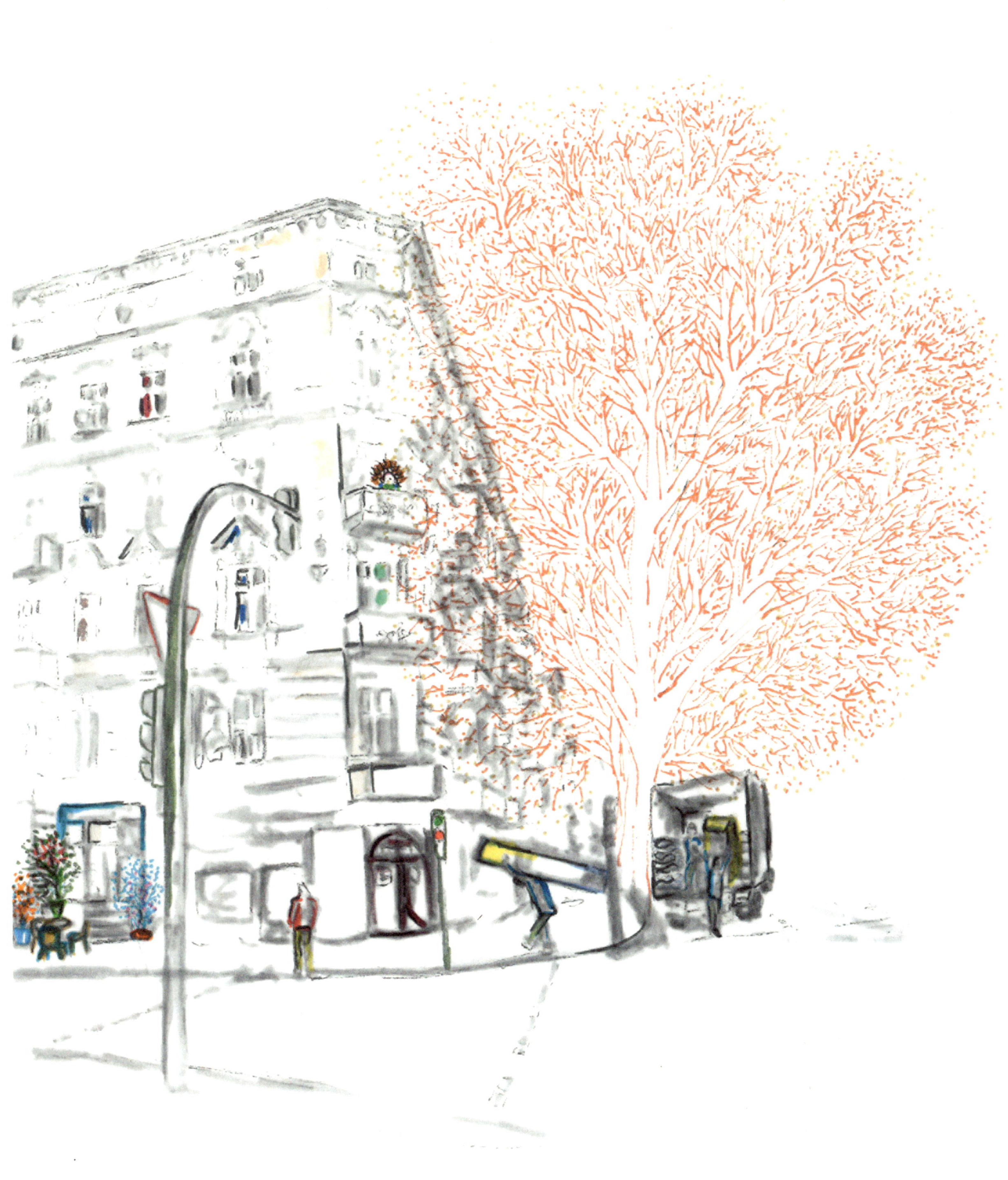

In Berlin ist alles fremd für sie:

die Plätze,

Everything in Berlin is unfamiliar to her:

the city squares,

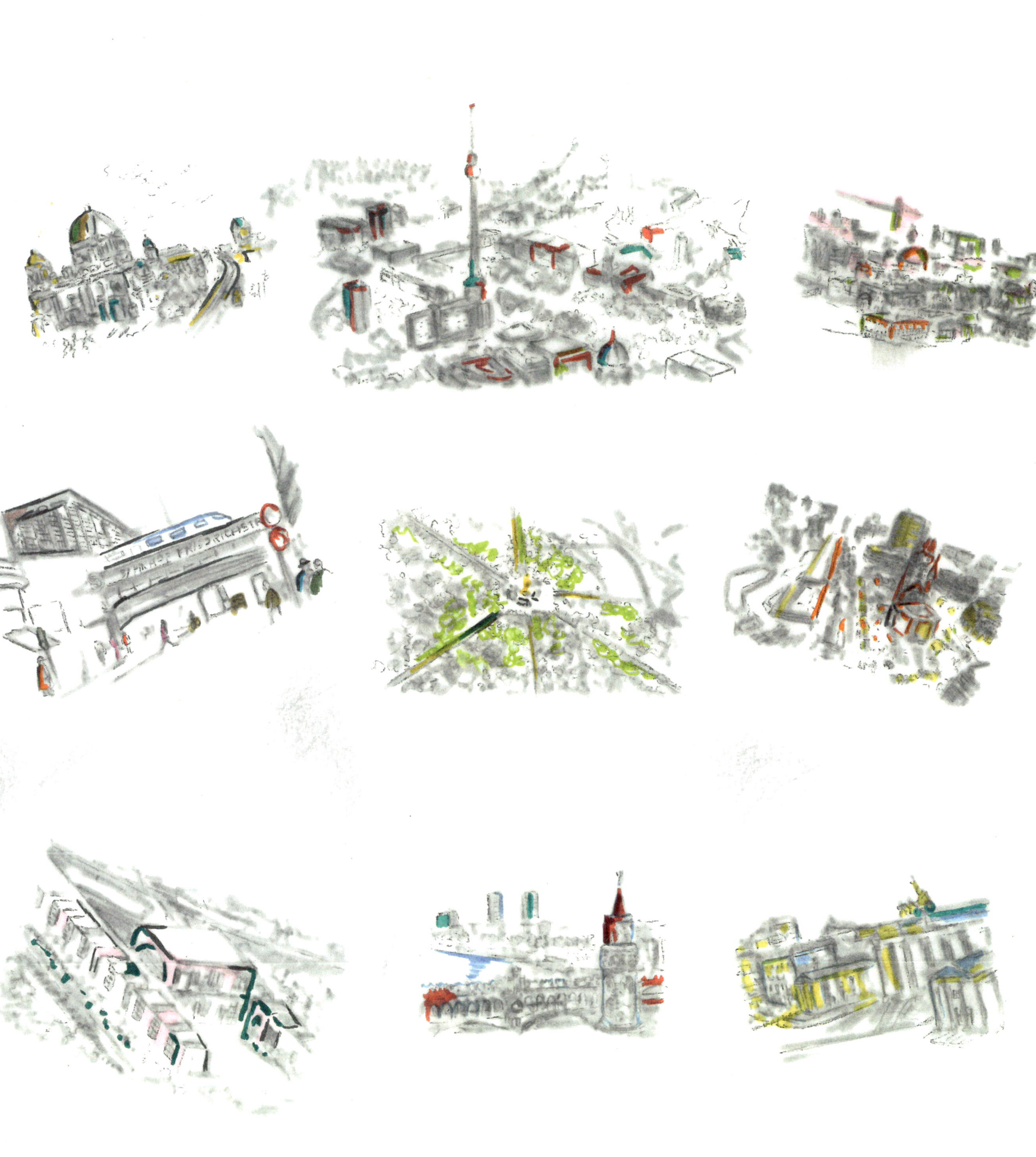
FRIEDRICHSTR

die Häuser,

the buildings,

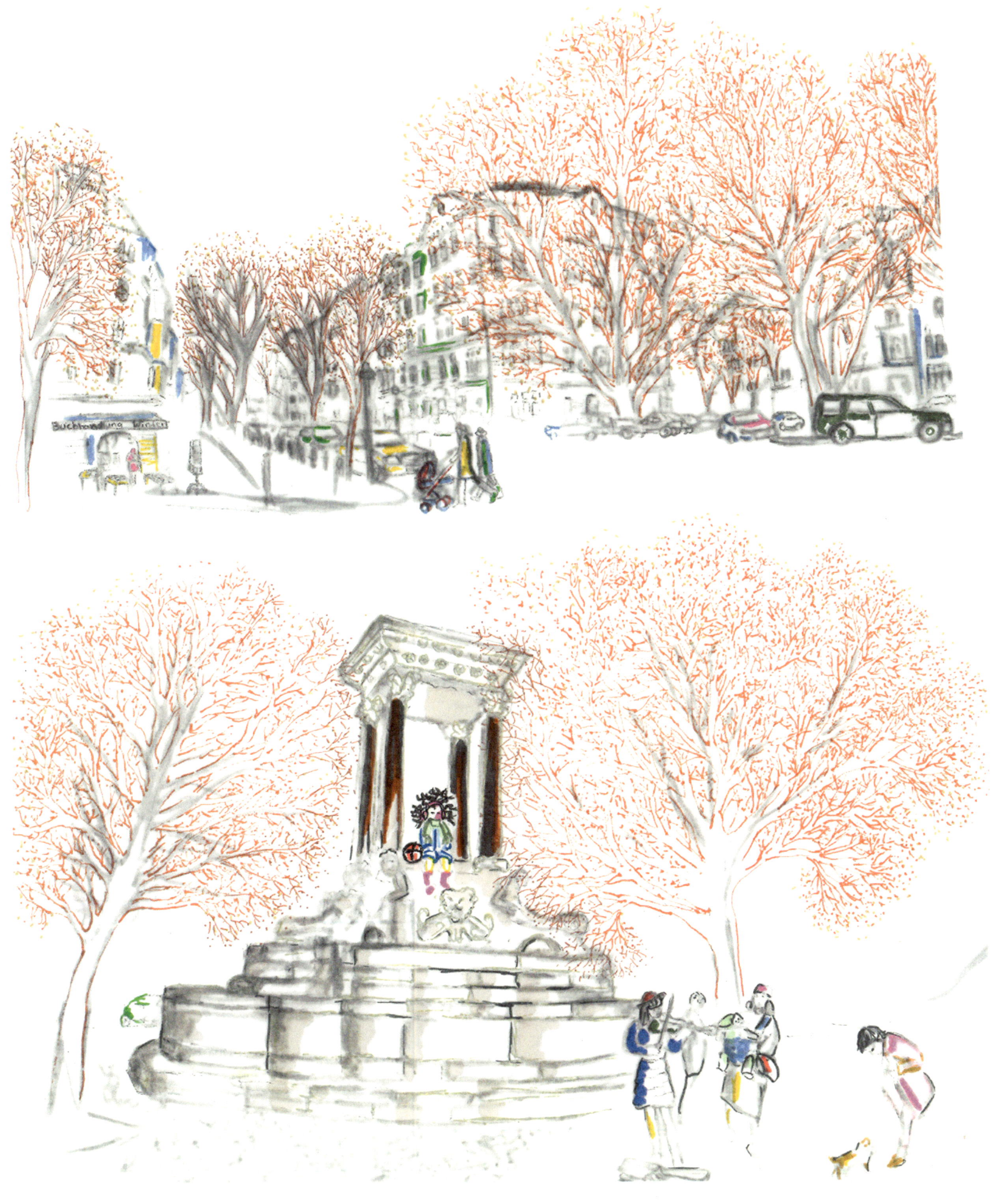
Buchhandlung Wieser

die Strassen,

the streets,

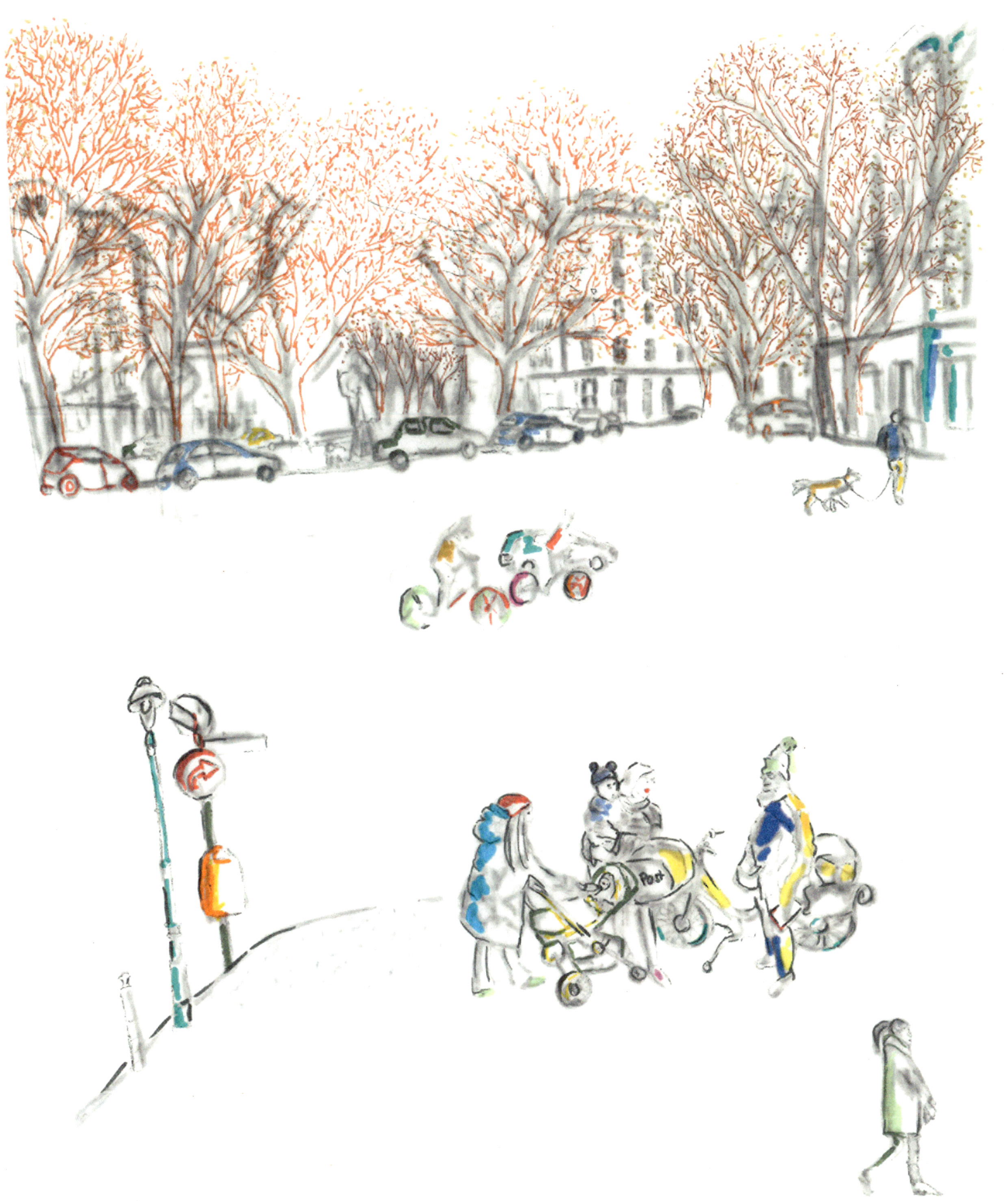

der Spielplatz.

the playground.

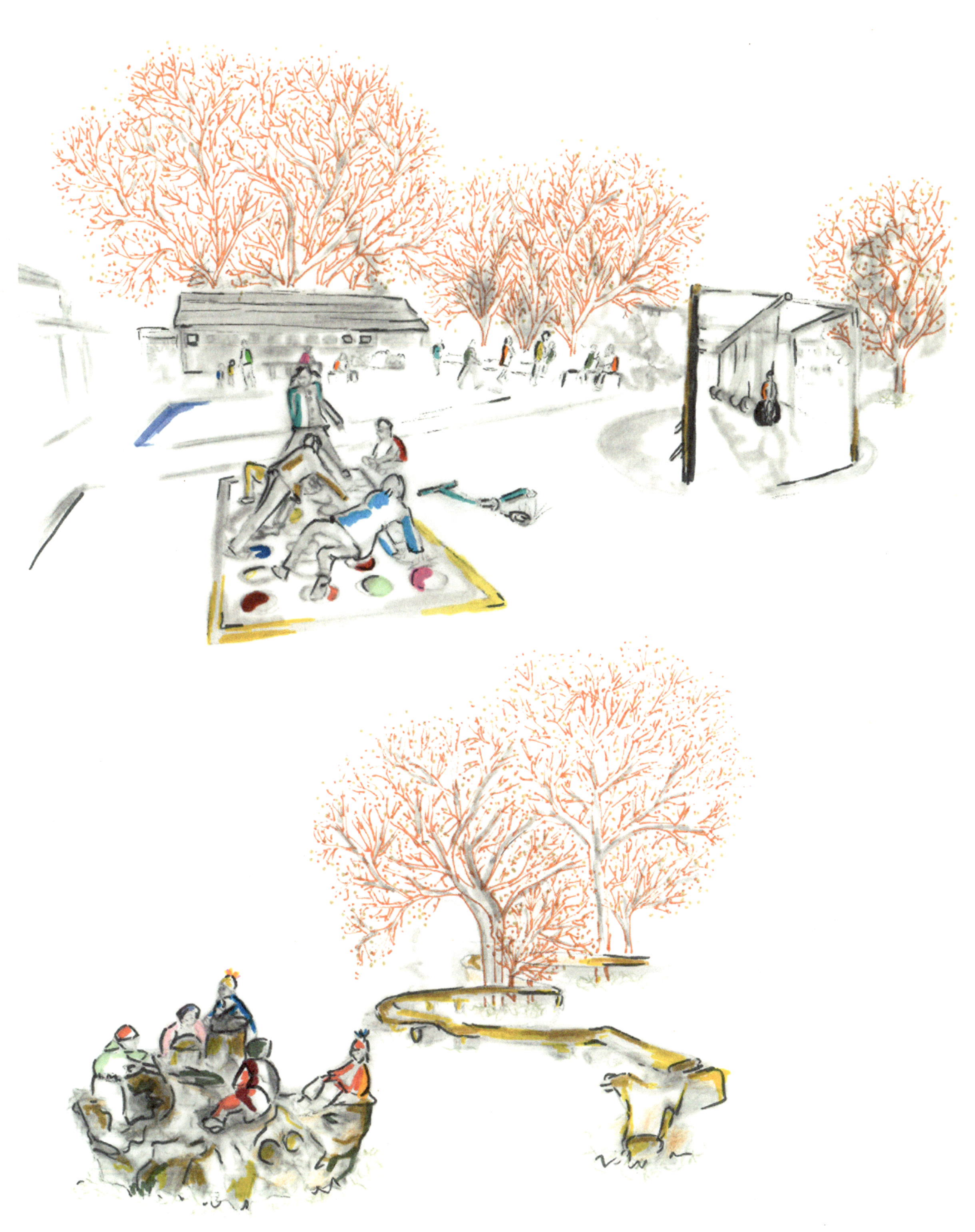

Vor allem die neue Schule ist ihr ganz fremd,
so dass es ihr schwer fällt, sich zurechtzufinden.
Elham fühlt sich von den anderen Kindern
beobachtet, und das macht sie sehr unsicher.
In der Pause sitzt sie mit ihrem Lieblingsball,
den sie von ihrer besten Münchner Freundin
Lara bekommen hat, allein auf einer Bank.

And most importantly, her new school is
completely unfamiliar to her, so it's hard for
her to find her way around. Elham feels the
other kids are watching her and that makes
her very insecure. During recess she sits
on a bench all by herself with her favorite
ball, which she got from Lara, her best friend
back in Munich.

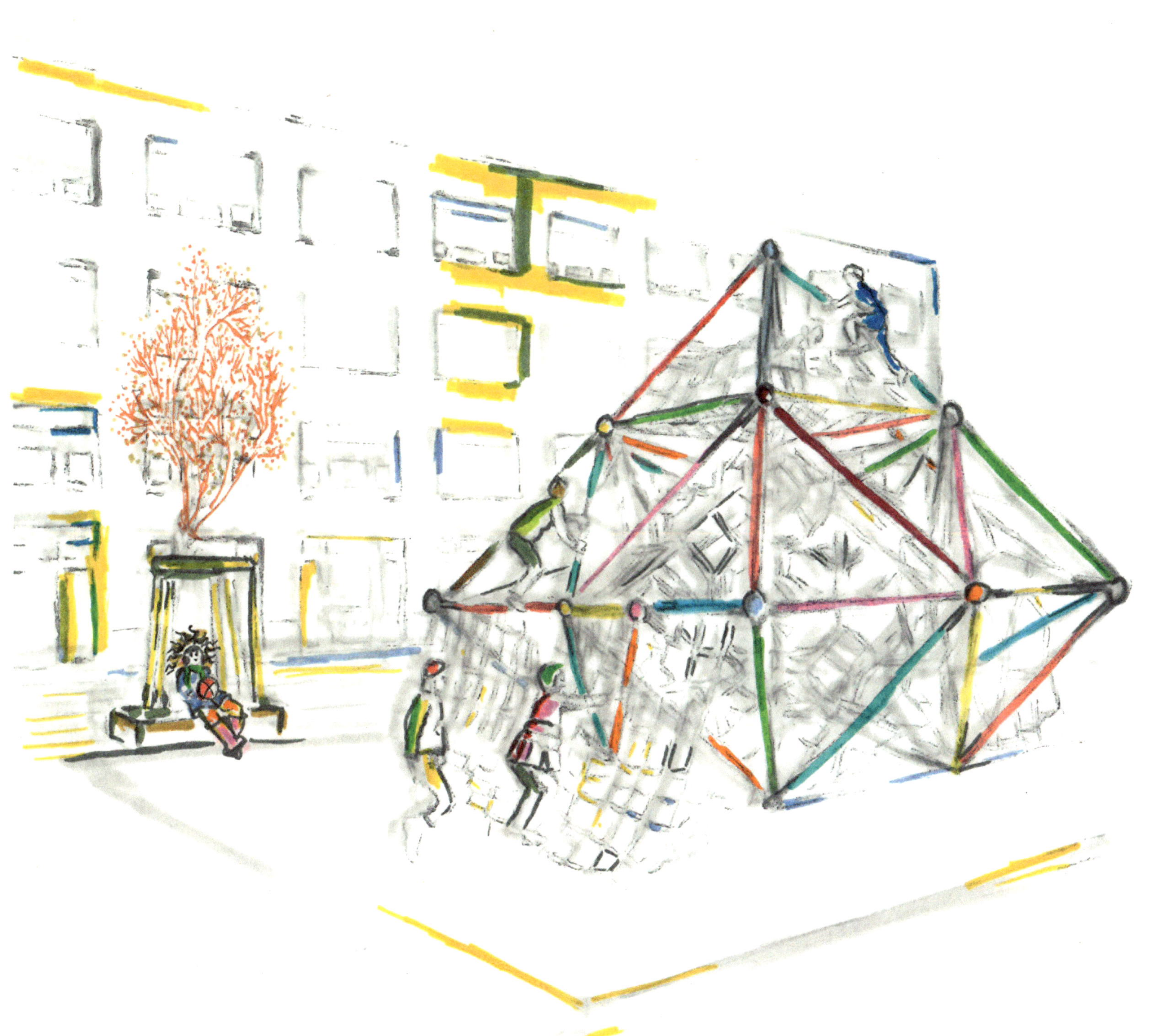

Eines Abends sagt Elham zu ihrer Mutter:
„Ich habe keine Lust, morgen in die Schule
zu gehen. Niemand will mit mir spielen!"
„Du kannst den Ball doch so hoch werfen",
antwortet ihre Mutter, „wenn die anderen
Kinder das sehen, werden sie ganz bestimmt
mit dir spielen wollen. Sei nicht traurig Elham,
du wirst sicher bald neue Freunde finden."

One evening Elham says to her mother,
"I don't feel like going to school tomorrow.
Nobody wants to play with me!"
"You can throw your ball so high up in the air,"
her mother says. "When the other kids see
that, they'll definitely want to play with you.
Don't be sad, Elham. I'm sure you'll make
new friends soon."

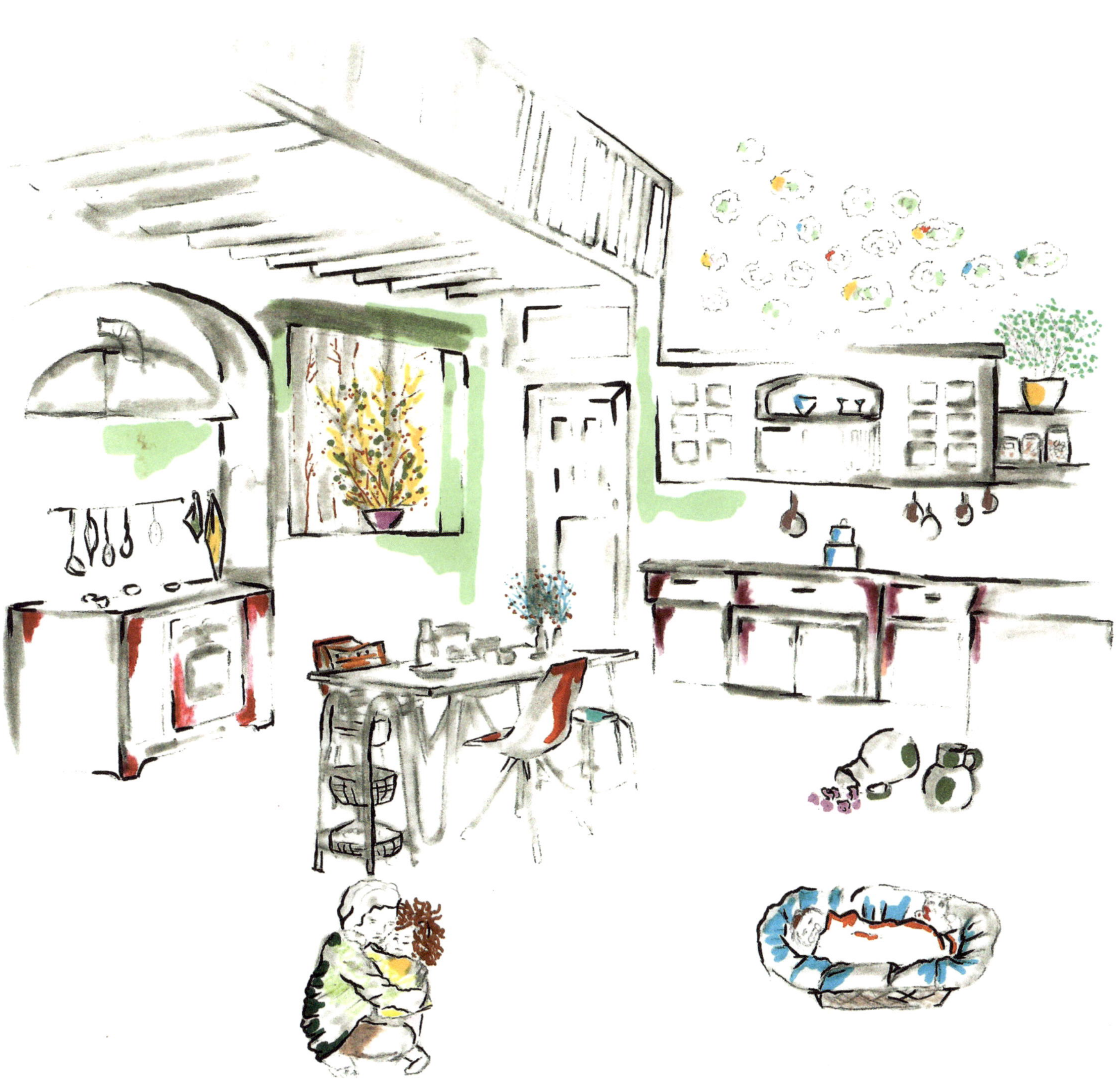

Am nächsten Tag nimmt sich Elham die Worte
ihrer Mama zu Herzen. In der Pause wirft sie
ihren Ball immer wieder in die Luft, hoch und
immer höher.

„Guckt mal, guckt mal, wie hoch Elham ihren
Ball werfen kann!" Neugierig eilen die anderen
Kinder herbei. „Dürfen wir mitspielen?"
Elham wirft den Ball einem Mädchen zu, und
bis zum Ende der Pause spielen sie zusammen.
Alle versuchen, den Ball so hoch zu werfen
wie Elham, hoch und immer höher.

Elham takes her mother's words to heart. The
next day at school, during recess, she throws
her ball up again and again, higher and higher
up into the air.

"Look! Look how high Elham can throw her ball!"
Awestruck, her schoolmates rush over to watch.
"Can we play too?" Elham throws the ball to
one girl, and by the end of recess they're all
playing together. Everyone tries to throw the
ball up as high as Elham, and even higher.

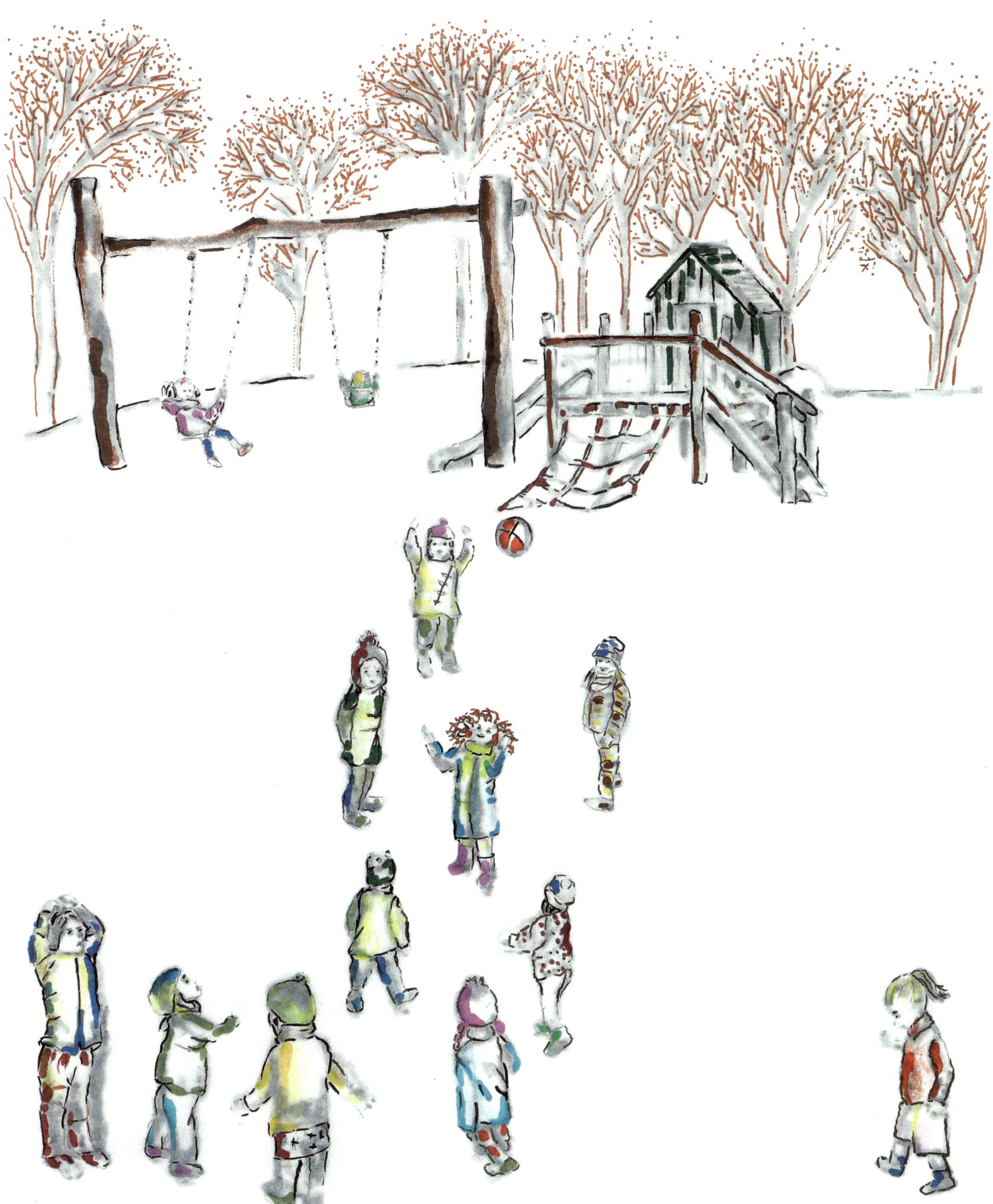

Zu Hause erzählt Elham ihrer Mutter glücklich
von ihrem Schultag: „Ich habe heute viele neue
Freunde gefunden! Ich habe mit meinem Ball
gespielt, ihn einfach hoch in die Luft geworfen,
und dann wollten die Kinder mitspielen.
Sie haben mich gefragt, wo ich herkomme, und
morgen spielen wir wieder zusammen!"

„Wie toll", sagt ihre Mutter glücklich, „ich bin
stolz auf dich, denn du hattest den Mut allein
zu spielen, und den anderen zu zeigen, wie
geschickt du mit deinem Ball bist! Ich wusste,
dass du es schaffst, schnell neue Freunde zu
finden!"

Elham comes home all excited and tells her
mother about her day at school: "I made lots
of new friends today! I played with my ball,
I just threw it high up into the air and then
the other kids wanted to play too. They asked
me where I'm from and tomorrow we're going
to play together again!"

"That's wonderful!" her mother exclaims happily.
"I'm so proud of you for having the courage
to play by yourself and show the others how
good you are at playing ball! I knew you'd
manage to make new friends in no time!"

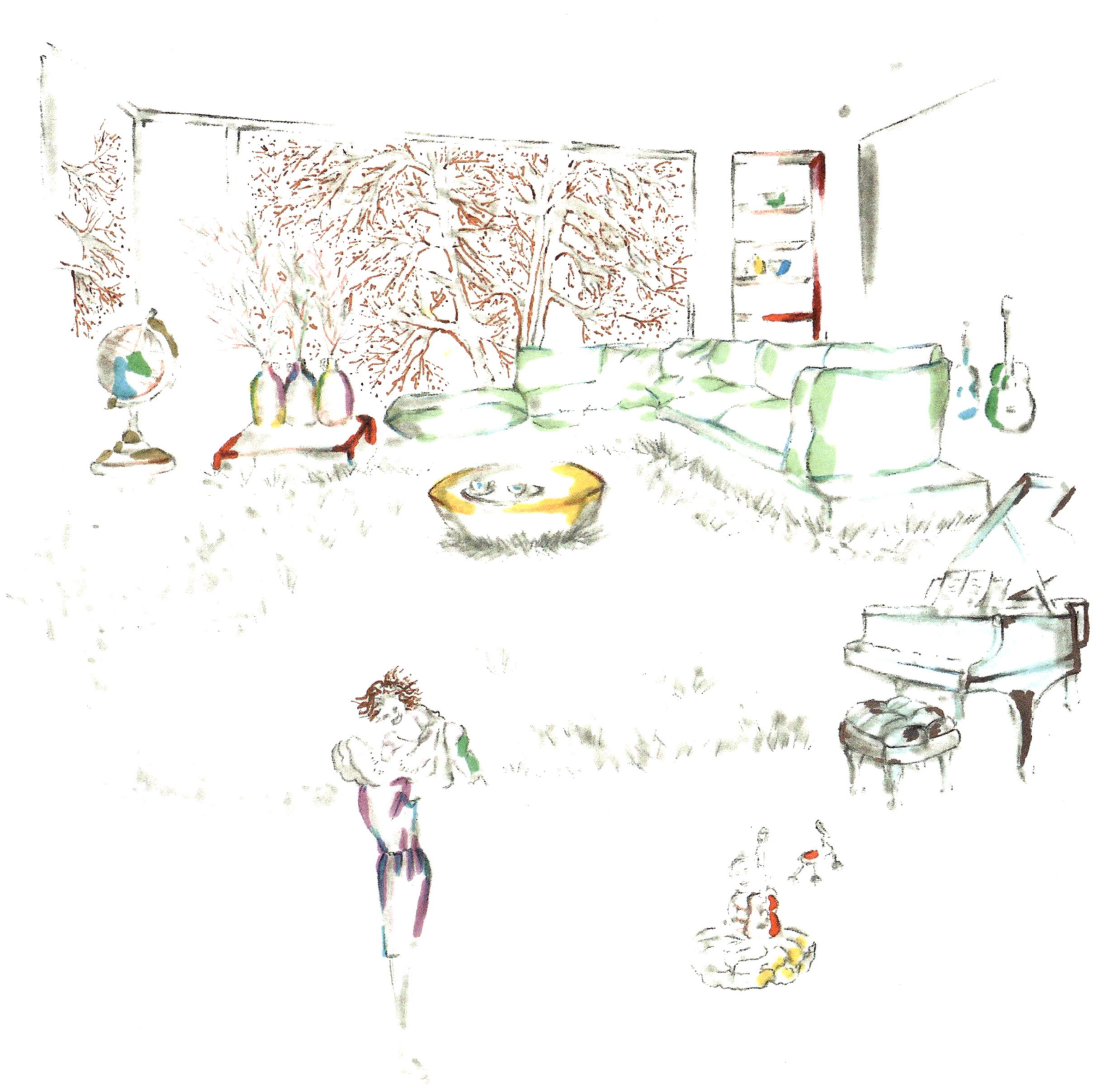

Am Abend in ihrem Zimmer freut sich Elham
schon auf den nächsten Schultag, wenn sie
ihre neuen Freunde wieder sieht und sie alle
zusammen spielen.

That evening in her room, Elham is already
looking forward to seeing all her new
friends at school the next day and playing
together again.

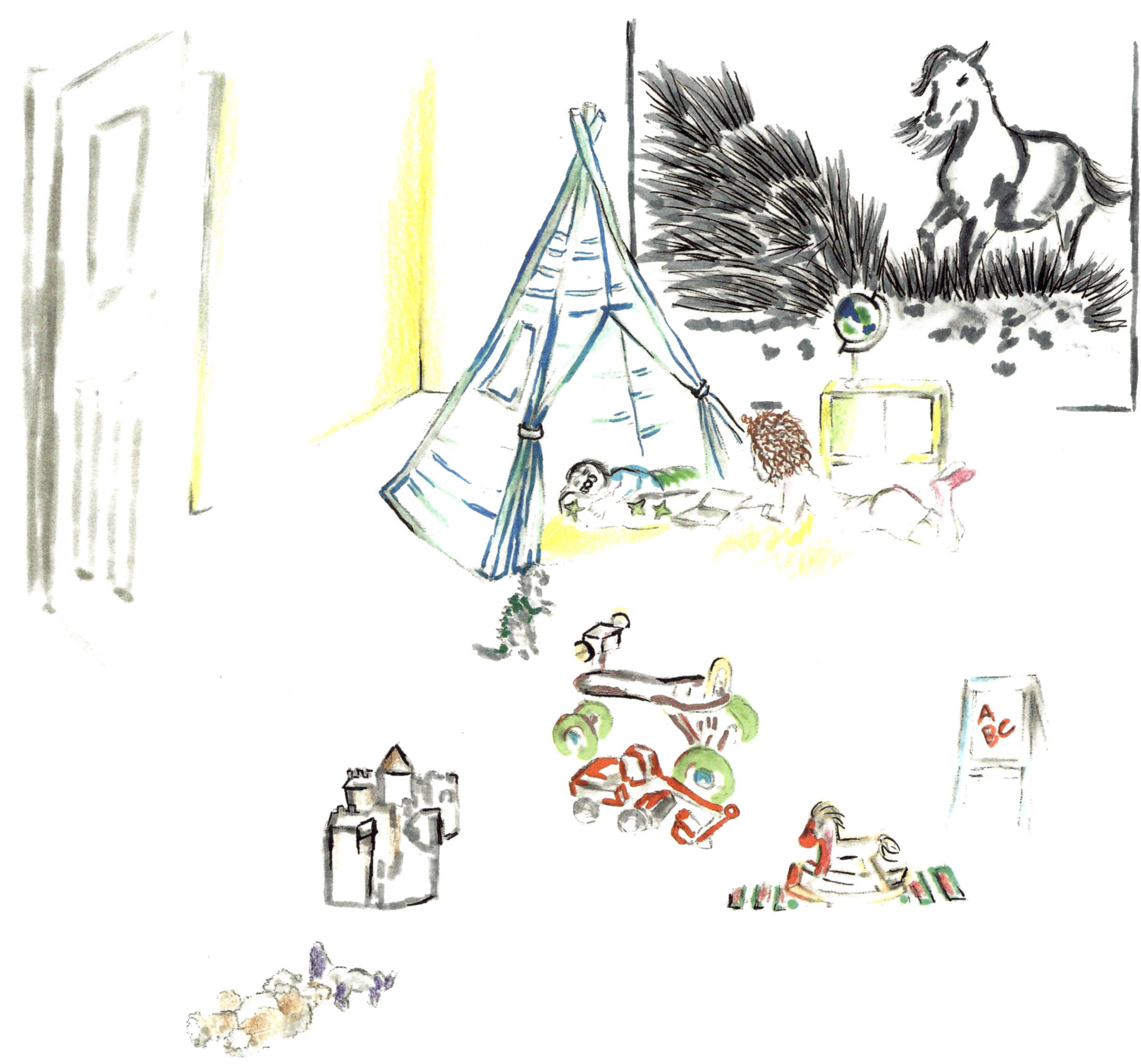

Bleib so grossartig, wie du bist!

Stay as great as you are!

Das ist Aylin. Sie ist vier Jahre alt und geht sehr
gerne in die Kita.

Ihr grösstes Vorbild ist ihr grosser Bruder Arian,
der Basketballspieler ist. Er hat ihr das Spiel
beigebracht. Vor einiger Zeit ist er nach Paris
gezogen, wo seine neue Mannschaft spielt.
Am Wochenende fährt Aylin mit ihrer Mama
Sevil nach Paris, um Arian spielen zu sehen,
und sie freut sich sehr darauf.

This is Aylin. She's four years old and really likes
going to kindergarten.

Her biggest role model is her big brother Arian.
He's a basketball player and he taught her how to
play the game. Some time ago he moved to Paris
to join a new basketball team. So Aylin's mama
is taking her to Paris on the weekend to see him
play, and she's very excited about that.

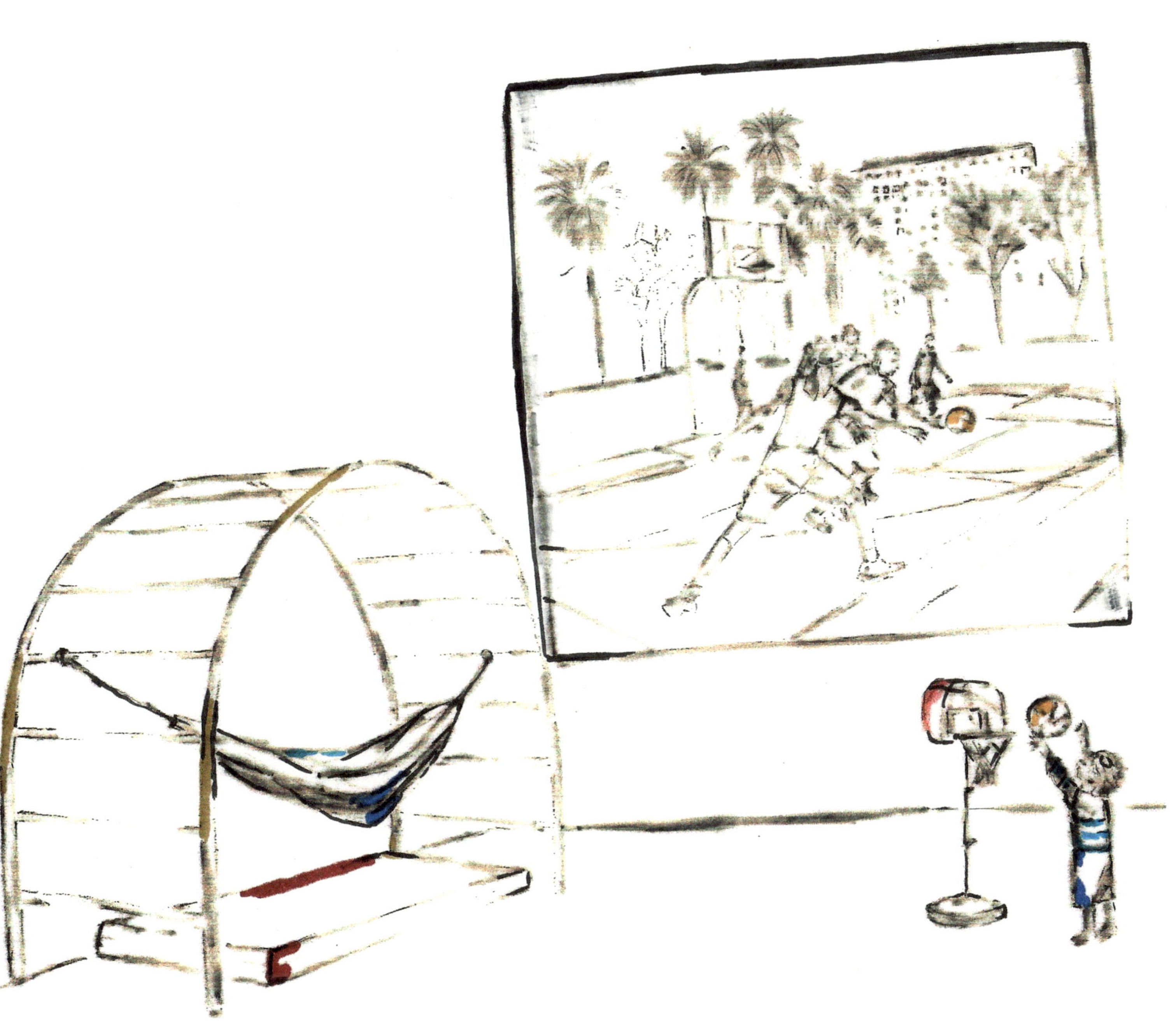

Endlich ist Freitag! In der Kita haben die Kinder
an diesem Nachmittag gemalt und nun alles
aufgeräumt. Aylin wartet ungeduldig auf ihre
Mama.

Friday at last! The children did drawings this
afternoon in kindergarten, now they're done
cleaning up. Aylin can't wait for her mama to
come.

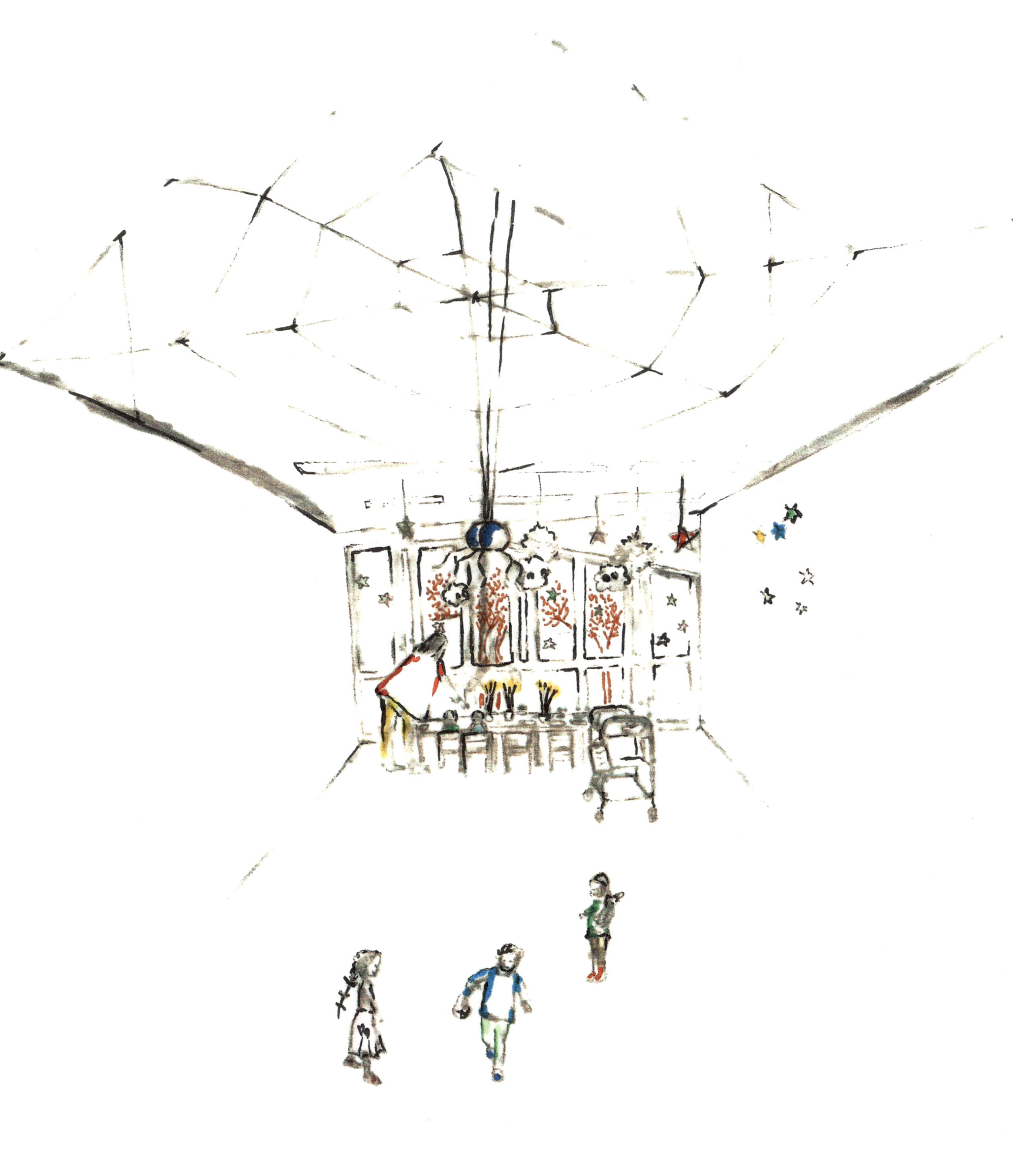

Sevil holt Aylin von der Kita ab. Eilig packen sie alles
zusammen, denn sie müssen den Zug rechtzeitig erwischen.

Pias Mutter Lisa beobachtet die beiden und fragt Sevil vor
allen anderen Eltern und Kindern: „Sag mal, Sevil, soll aus
deiner Tochter Peter Pan werden? Sie sieht ja aus wie ein
Junge!" Sevil antwortet: „Aylin kann ihre Haare tragen, wie
es ihr gefällt, und auch anziehen, was sie mag."

Da ruft Lisa aus: „Guckt mal, das ist wohl der Junge, den
sie sich immer gewünscht hat!"

„Ich habe mir immer eine glückliche Tochter gewünscht",
entgegnet Sevil, „und das ist Aylin." Und fügt angewidert
an: „Was Vorurteile betrifft, bist du mir ja ein schönes
Vorbild für deine Kinder!"

Aylin's mama, Sevil, has come to pick her up at kindergarten. They pack up her stuff in a hurry because they
have a train to catch.

Pia's mother, Lisa, is watching them. "Say, Sevil, is your
daughter the next Peter Pan?" she scoffs in front of
all the other parents and children. "She looks like a boy."

"Aylin can wear her hair any way she likes," Sevil replies,
"and dress any way she likes too."

"Look," Lisa jeers, "this must be the boy she's always wanted!"

"I've always wanted to have a happy daughter," Sevil says,
"and that's what Aylin is. You're a fine role model for your
kids with these stereotypes," she adds, disgusted.

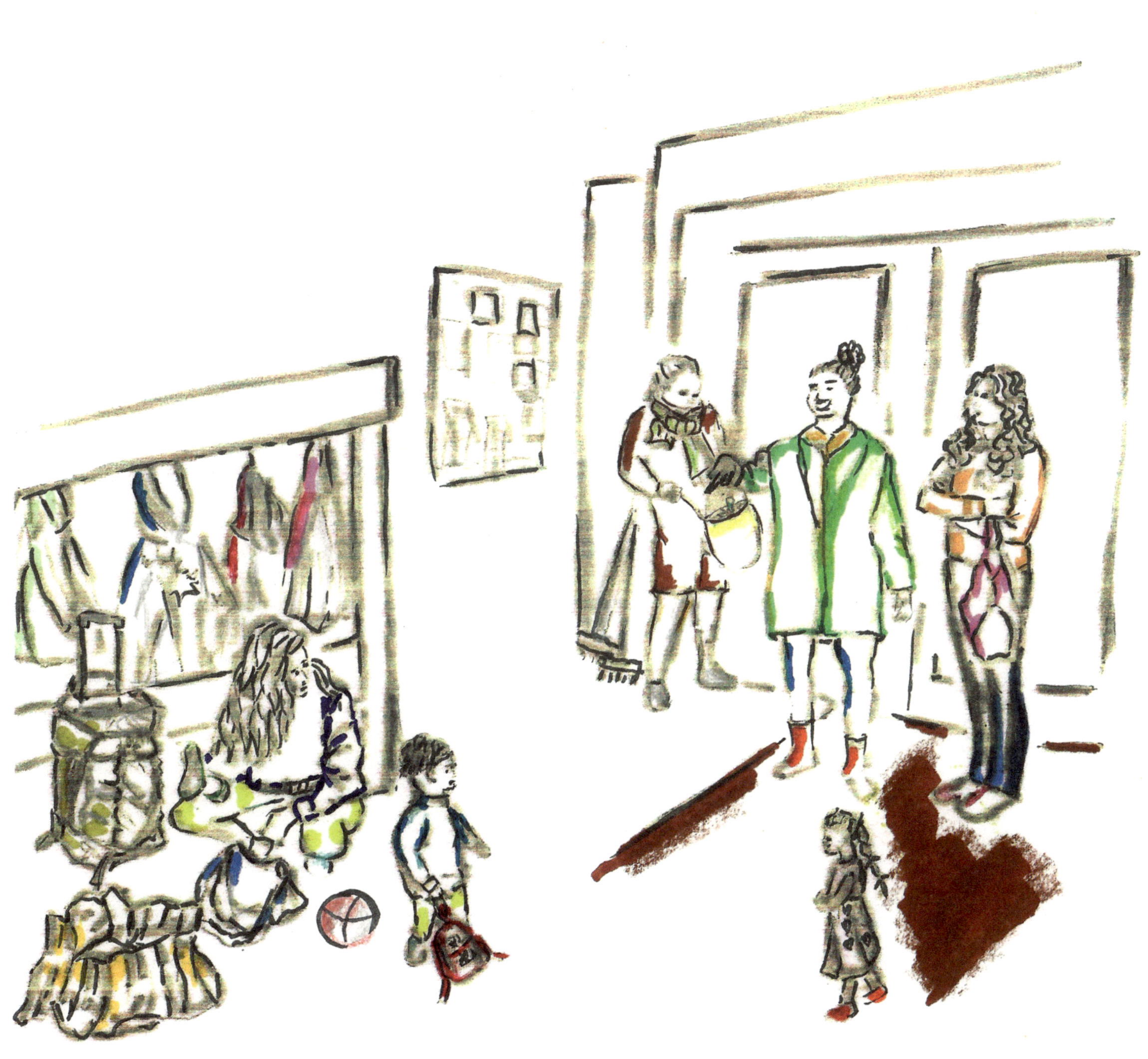

Hand in Hand verlassen Aylin und ihre
Mama die Kita in Richtung Bahnhof.
Endlich geht die Reise los!

Aylin and her mama leave the kindergarten
hand in hand and head for the station.
They're off at last!

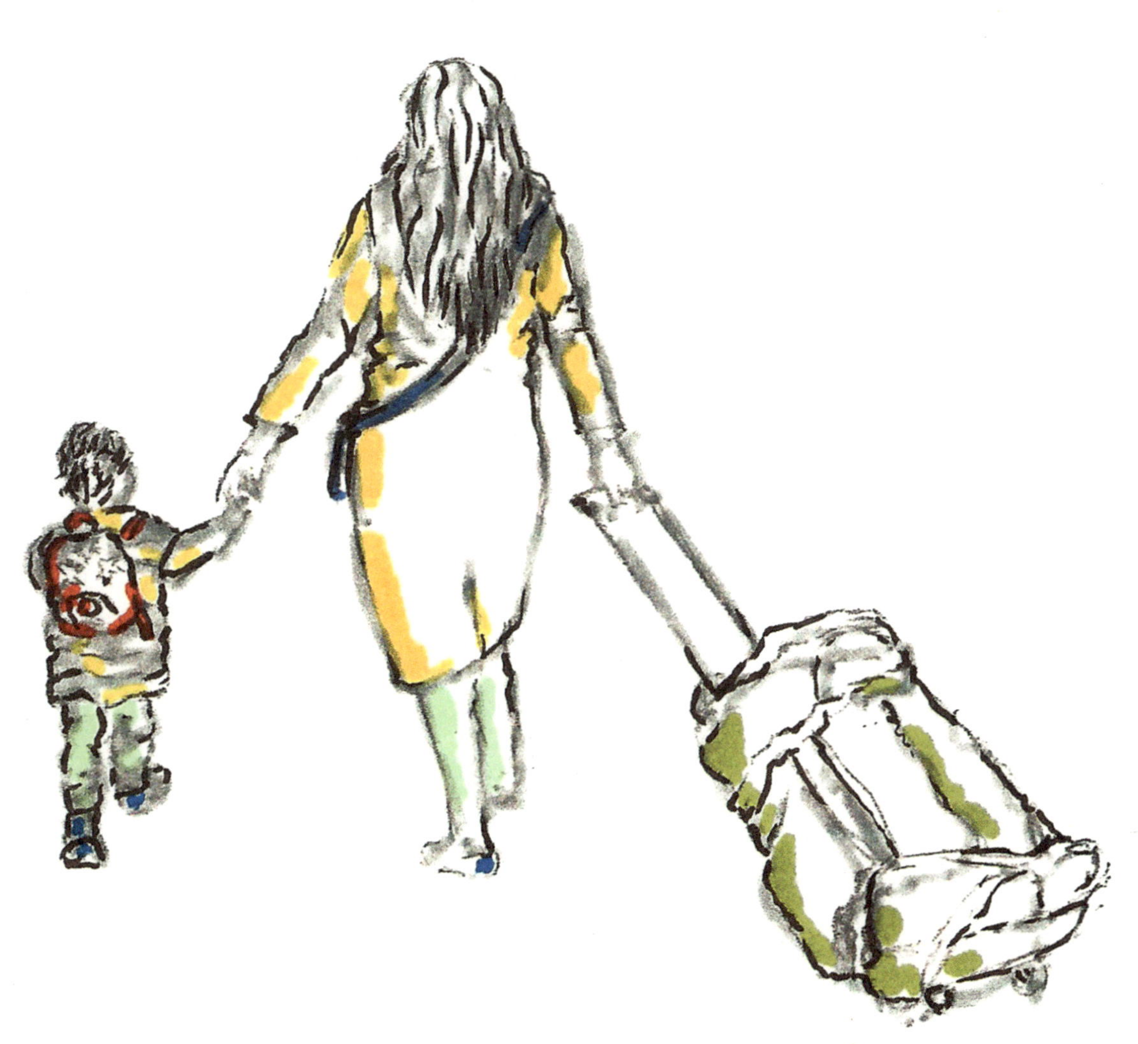

Auf der Zugfahrt freut sich Aylin schon
darauf, ihren grossen Bruder Arian bald
wiederzusehen.

On the train, Aylin is all excited about seeing
her big brother again.

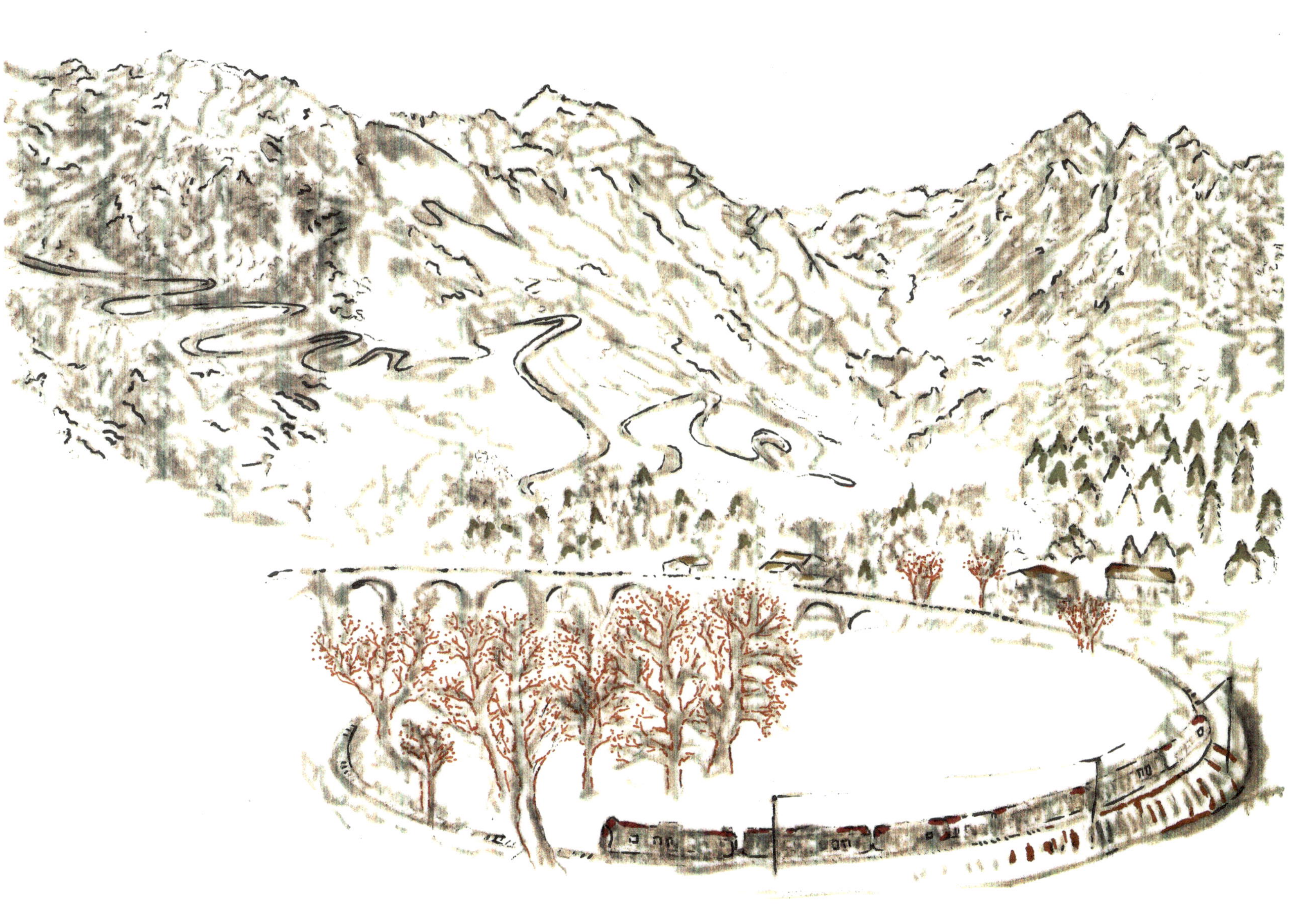

In Paris angekommen, kann Aylin ihre Freude
kaum noch zurückhalten! Fröhlich schwingt sie
den mitgebrachten Basketball in der Tasche hin
und her. Sogleich fahren sie zur Sporthalle, wo
das Spiel von Arians Mannschaft stattfindet.

When they get to Paris, Aylin is so happy she
can hardly contain herself anymore! She has
brought a basketball with her in a bag, which
she now swings gleefully back and forth. They
head straight to the arena where Arian's team
is playing a match.

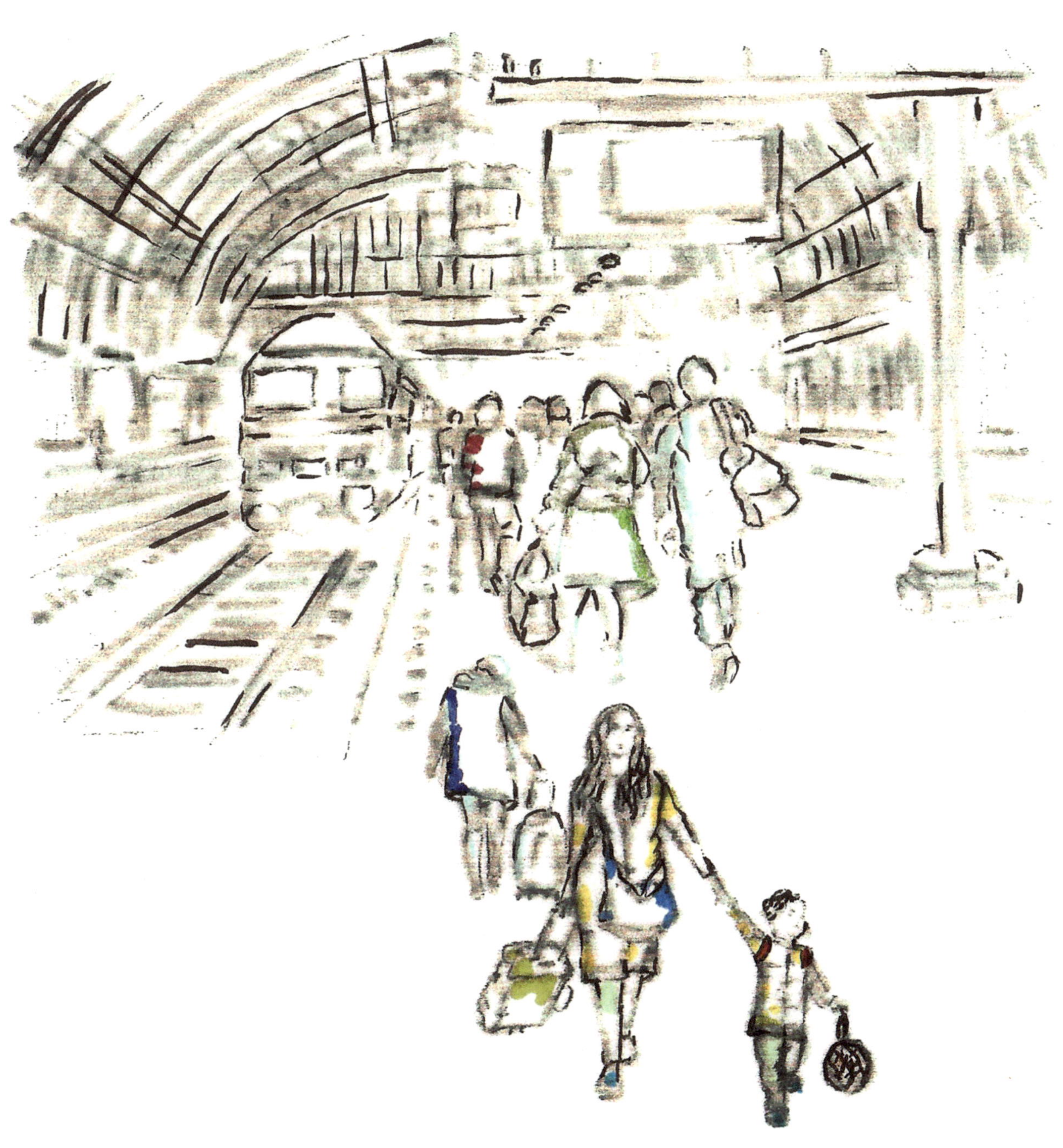

Nun ist es endlich so weit: Das Spiel geht los!

Now it's finally time for the game to begin!

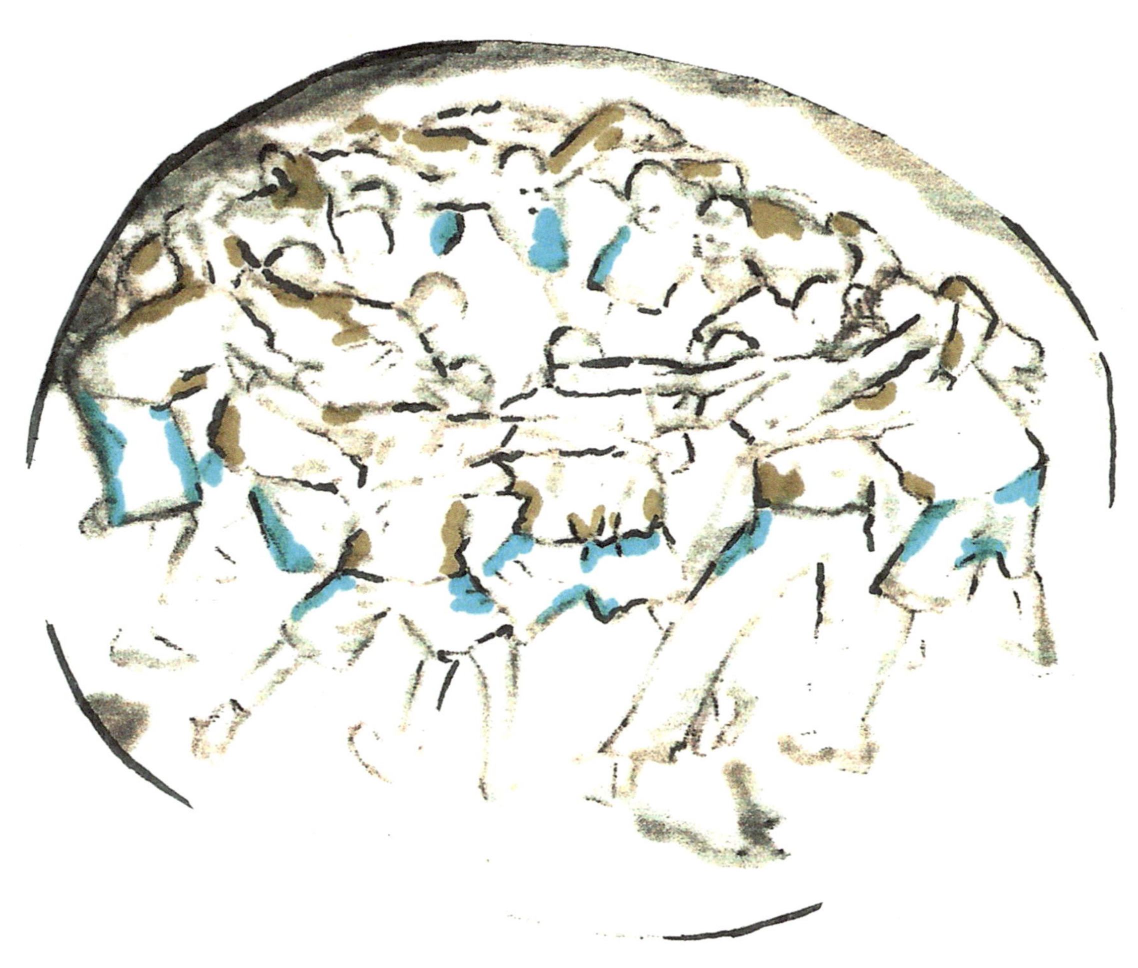

Arians Mannschaft spielt überlegen.

Arian's team plays better.

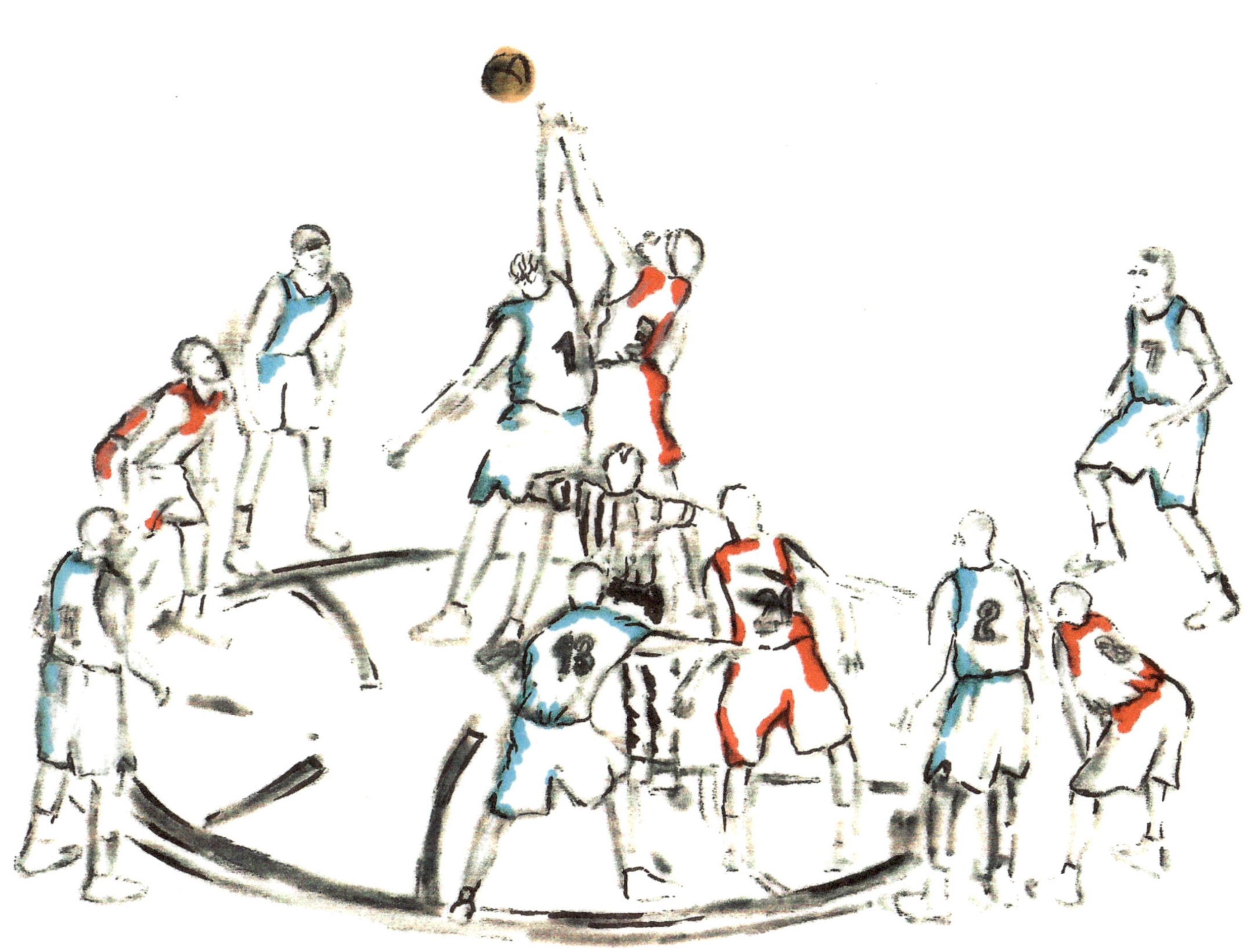

Aylin ist stolz auf ihren grossen Bruder,
der einen Korb nach dem anderen wirft.

Aylin is so proud of her big brother, who
shoots one basket after another.

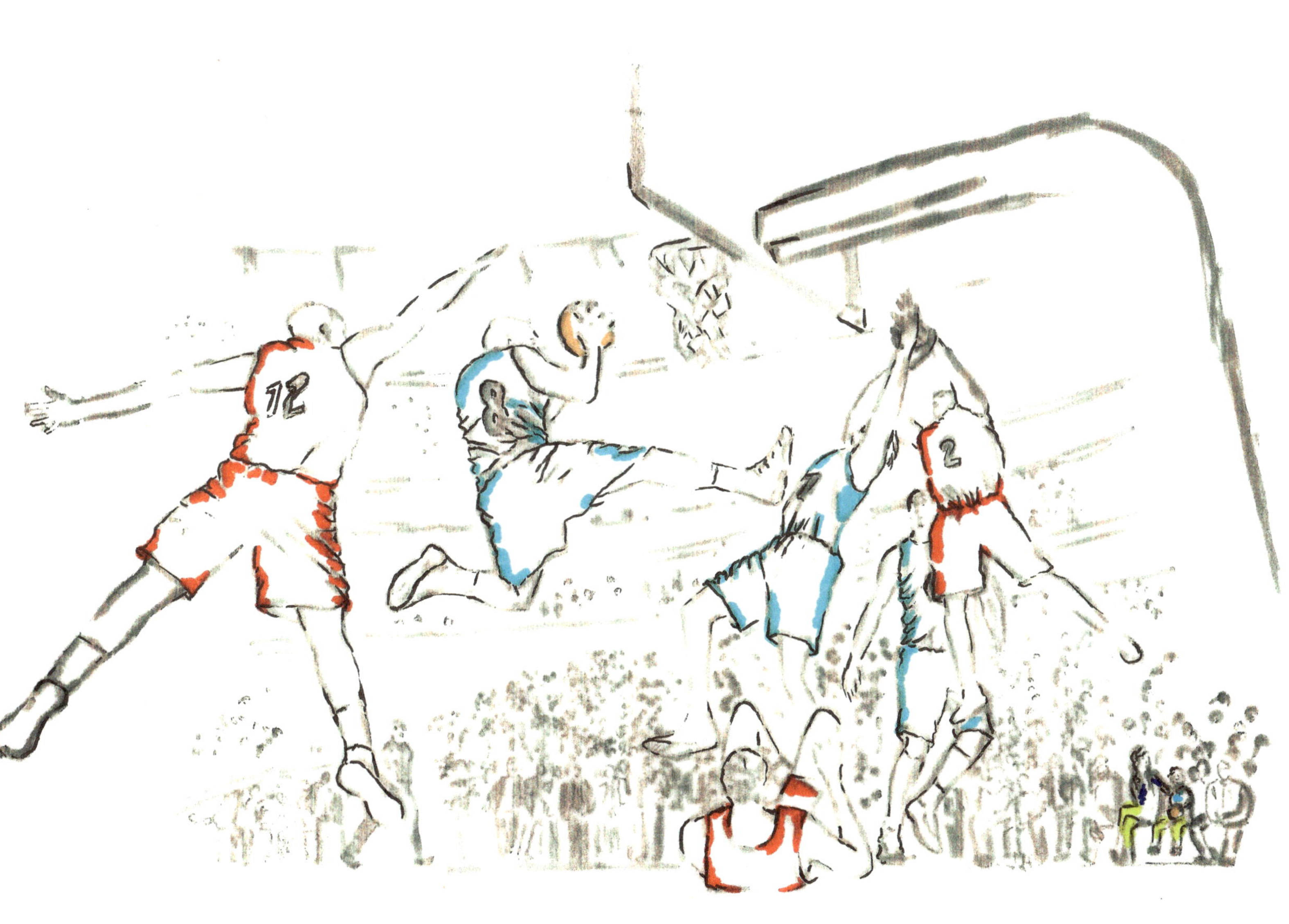

Die Mannschaft holt Punkt um Punkt...

His team racks up the points...

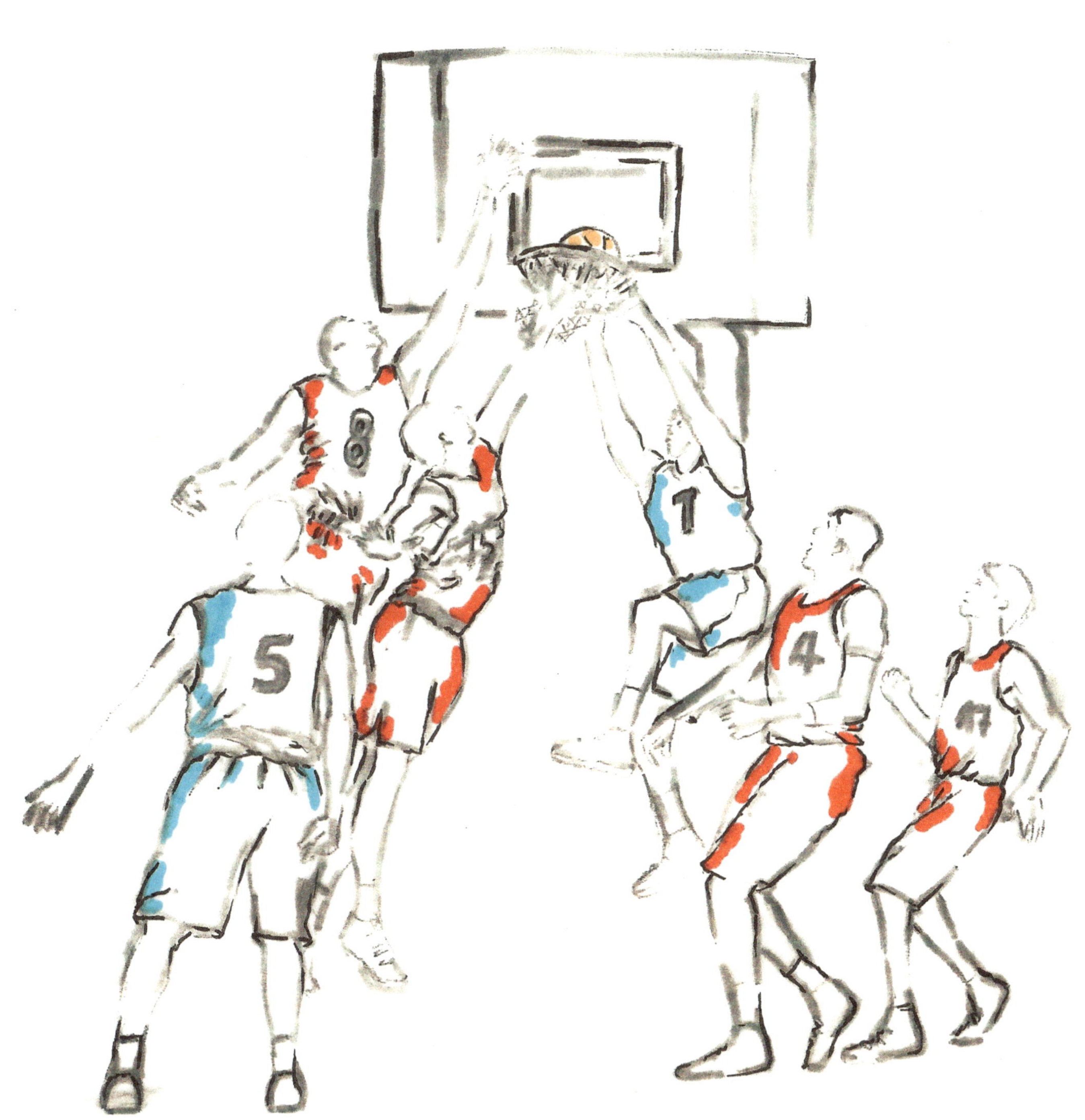
8
5
1
4

und gewinnt das Spiel!

and wins the game!

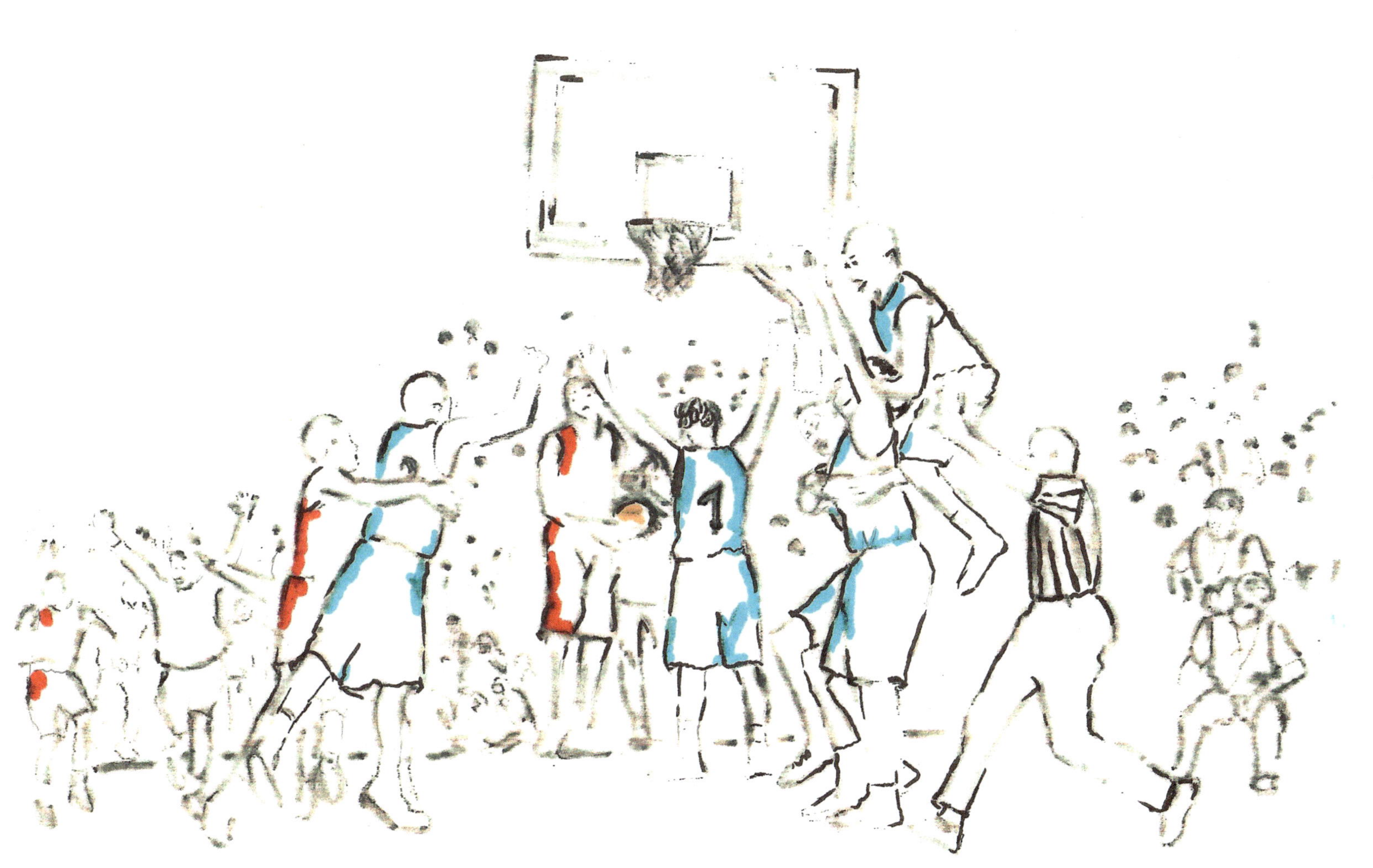

Der Sieg muss gefeiert werden, sie gehen alle zusammen
essen. Arian fällt auf, dass seine kleine Schwester kaum
etwas isst und fragt: „Aylin, ist alles in Ordnung mit dir?
Bist du traurig?"
Da erzählt Aylin von Pias Mutter Lisa, und wie sie sich
über ihr Aussehen lustig gemacht hat. „Ich habe Angst,
am Montag wieder in die Kita zu gehen! Vielleicht wird
Pias Mutter wieder so gemeine Dinge zu mir sagen."

Arian nimmt seine kleine Schwester auf den Schoss
und tröstet sie: „Achte nicht auf Dinge, die Menschen wie
Lisa unüberlegt sagen. Ich denke, in Wahrheit ist sie ein
trauriger Mensch der glaubt, sich besser zu fühlen, wenn
er andere lächerlich macht. Eigentlich kann sie einem
nur leid tun."

Aylin sagt: „Ich gehe gerne in die Kita, und ich spiele
auch gern mit Pia!"

This victory calls for a celebration, so they all go out for
dinner together. Noticing that his little sister has hardly
touched her food, Arian asks, "Aylin, is everything all
right with you? Are you sad?"

So Aylin tells him about Pia's mother, Lisa, and how she
made fun of her looks. "I'm afraid to go back to kindergarten on Monday. Pia's mother might say such mean
things to me again."

Arian takes his little sister on his lap and comforts her:
"Don't pay any attention to things people like Lisa say
without thinking. I bet she's actually a sad person who
thinks it makes her feel better to make fun of others.
Actually, we ought to feel sorry for her."

"I like going to kindergarten," Aylin says, "and I also like
playing with Pia!"

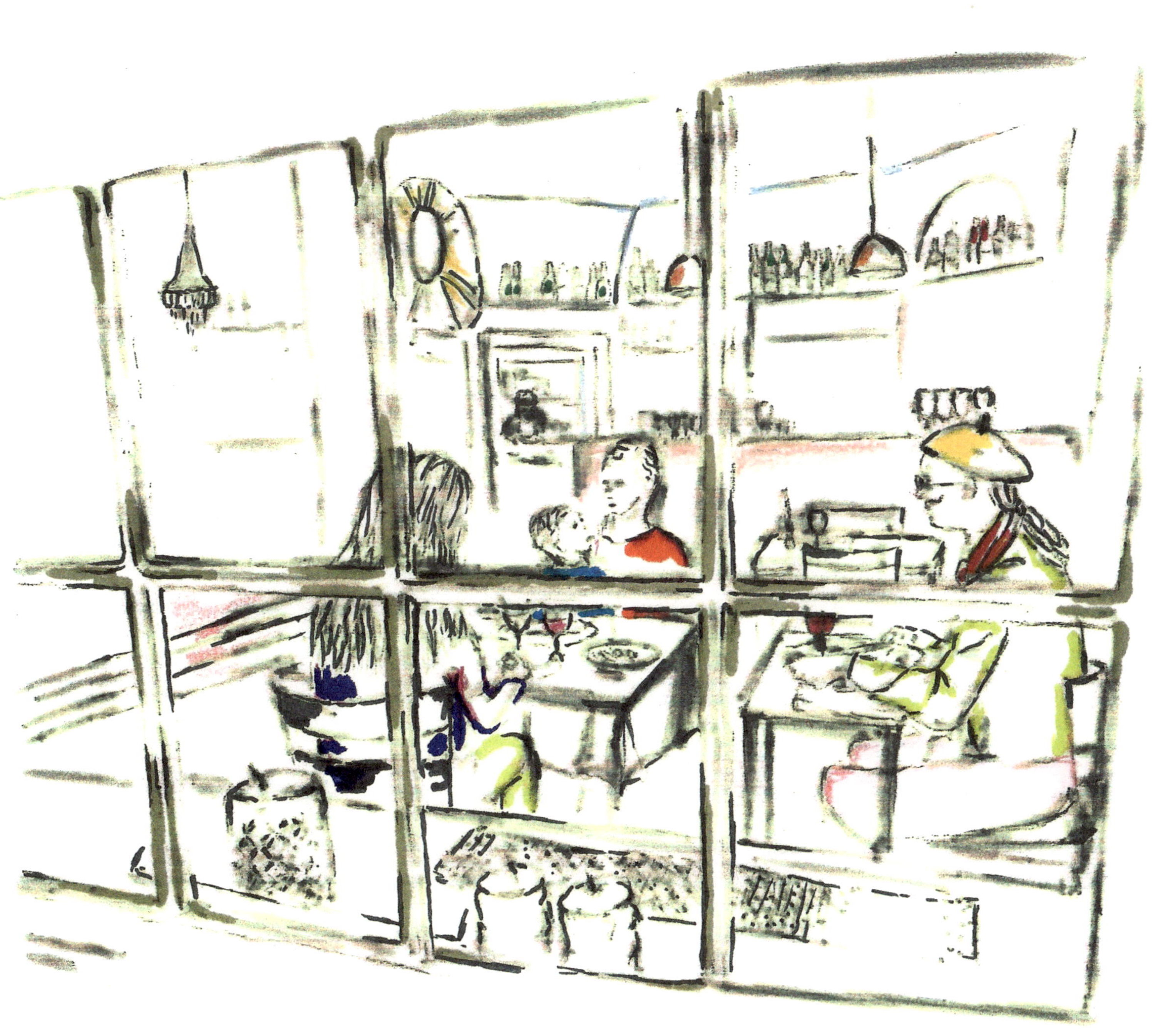

„Bleib einfach so liebenswert und freundlich,
wie du bist, Aylin! Steh zu dem, was du bist und
was du willst! Sei immer du selbst, dann kannst
du nur gewinnen, so wie ich. Versprochen?"

„Versprochen!", antwortet Aylin.

Aylin wird sich Arians Worte zu Herzen nehmen.

"Just stay as friendly and lovable as you are, Aylin!
Stand by who you are and what you want!
Always be yourself - then you'll be a winner, like me.
Promise?"

"Promise!" says Aylin.

Aylin takes Arian's words to heart.

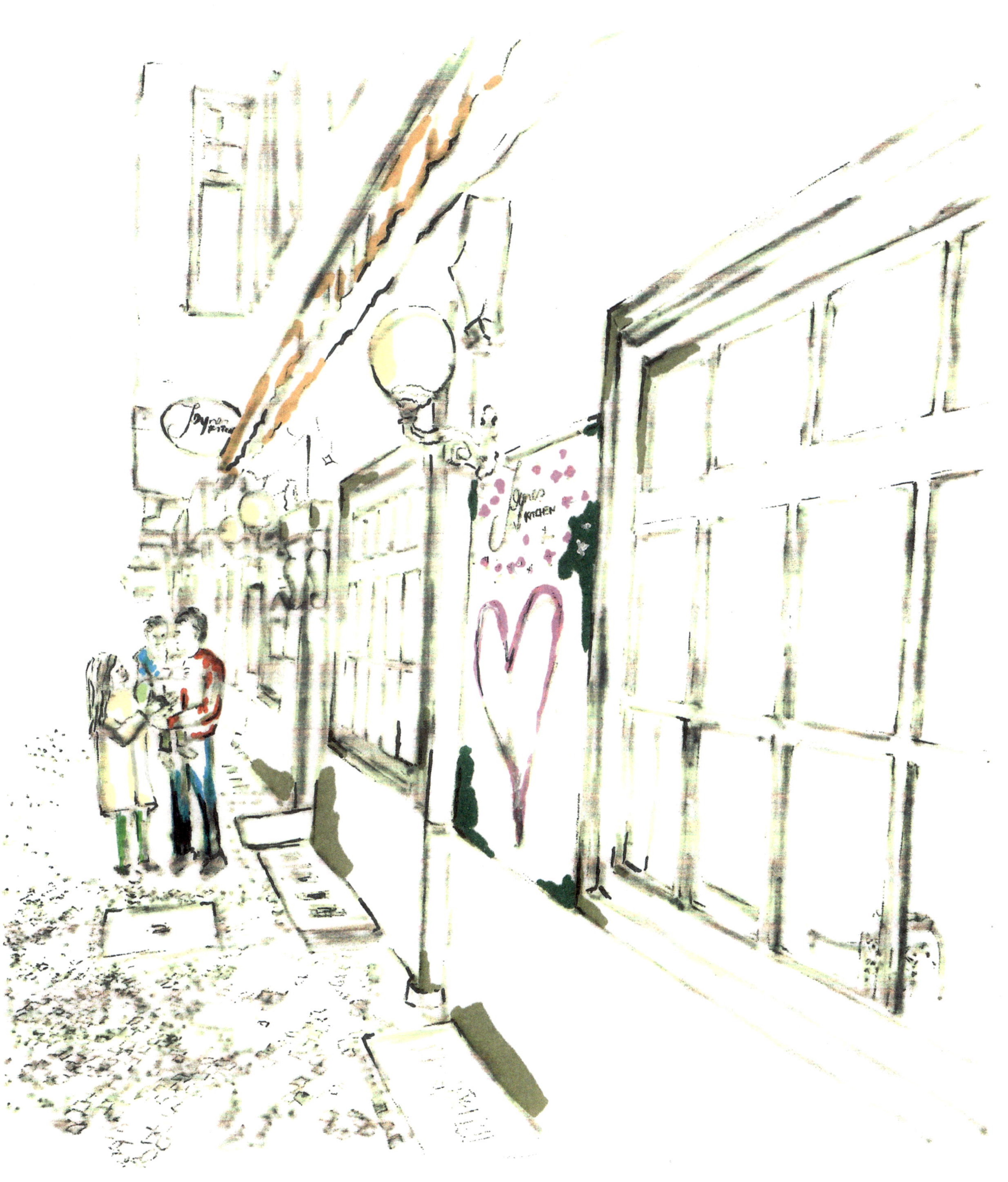

Glücklich spaziert sie mit Sevil und Arian durch
die Strassen von Paris, und sie freut sich darauf,
ihre Freunde am Montag in der Kita wiederzusehen.

Walking happily down the streets of Paris with
her mama and big brother, she can't wait to see her
friends again on Monday in kindergarten.

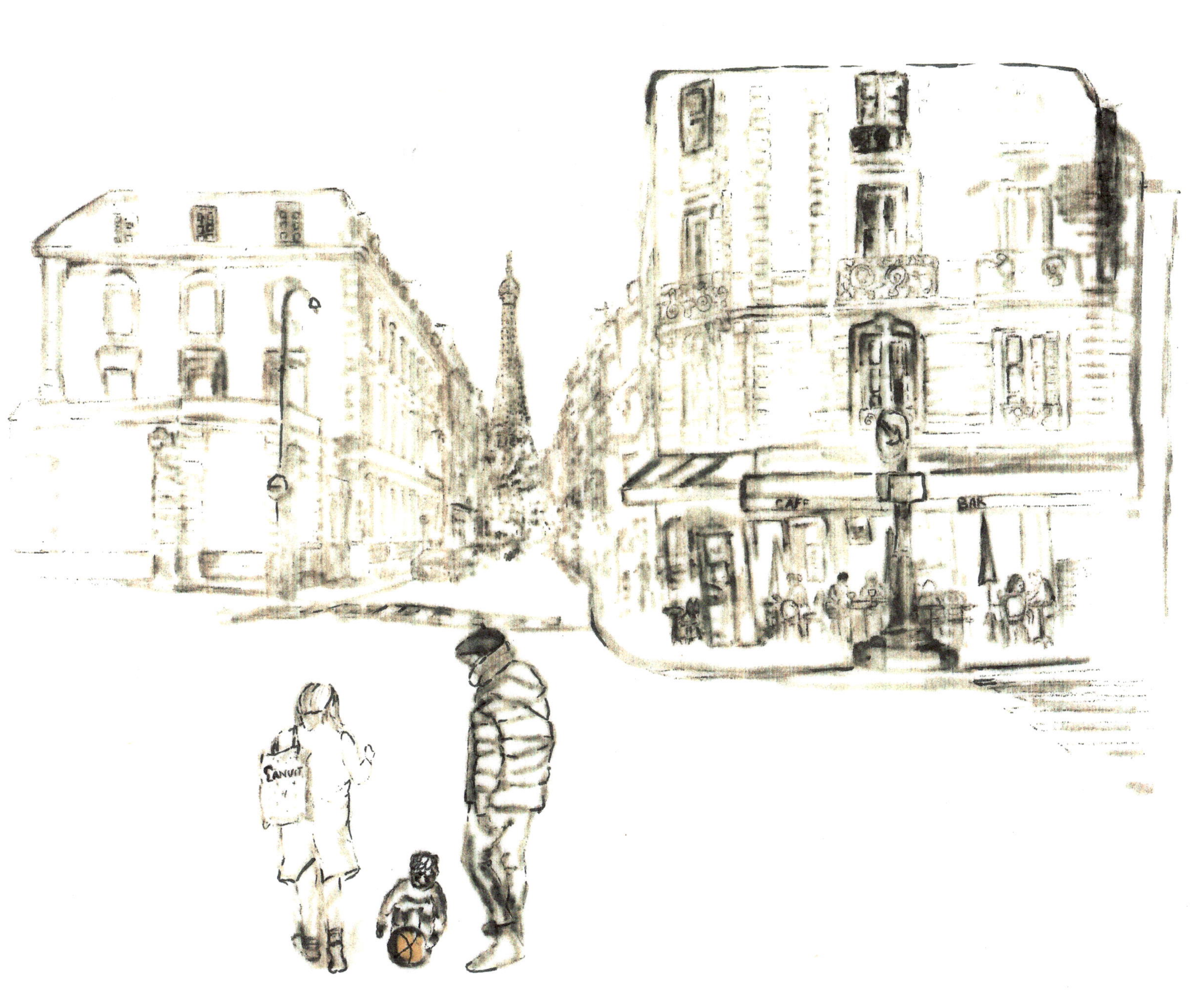

CAFÉ
BAR
Sanuit

Das fliegende Boot

The Flying Boat

Das sind die Geschwister Jakob, Sophia und
Jonathan mit ihrer Oma Assal. Sie sind sieben,
sechs und vier Jahre alt. Ihre verstorbene Mutter
Louise nannte sie liebevoll „meine drei mutigen
Löwenkinder". Sie war unheilbar krank und
musste vor einiger Zeit die Erde verlassen, um
an den Ort der Ewigkeit zu ziehen.

Jakob, Sophia and Jonathan are seven, six and
four years old. Here they are with their grandma,
Assal. Their mama, Louise, who used to call
them affectionately "my three brave lion cubs",
was terminally ill and had to leave this world
for the Everafter a few years ago.

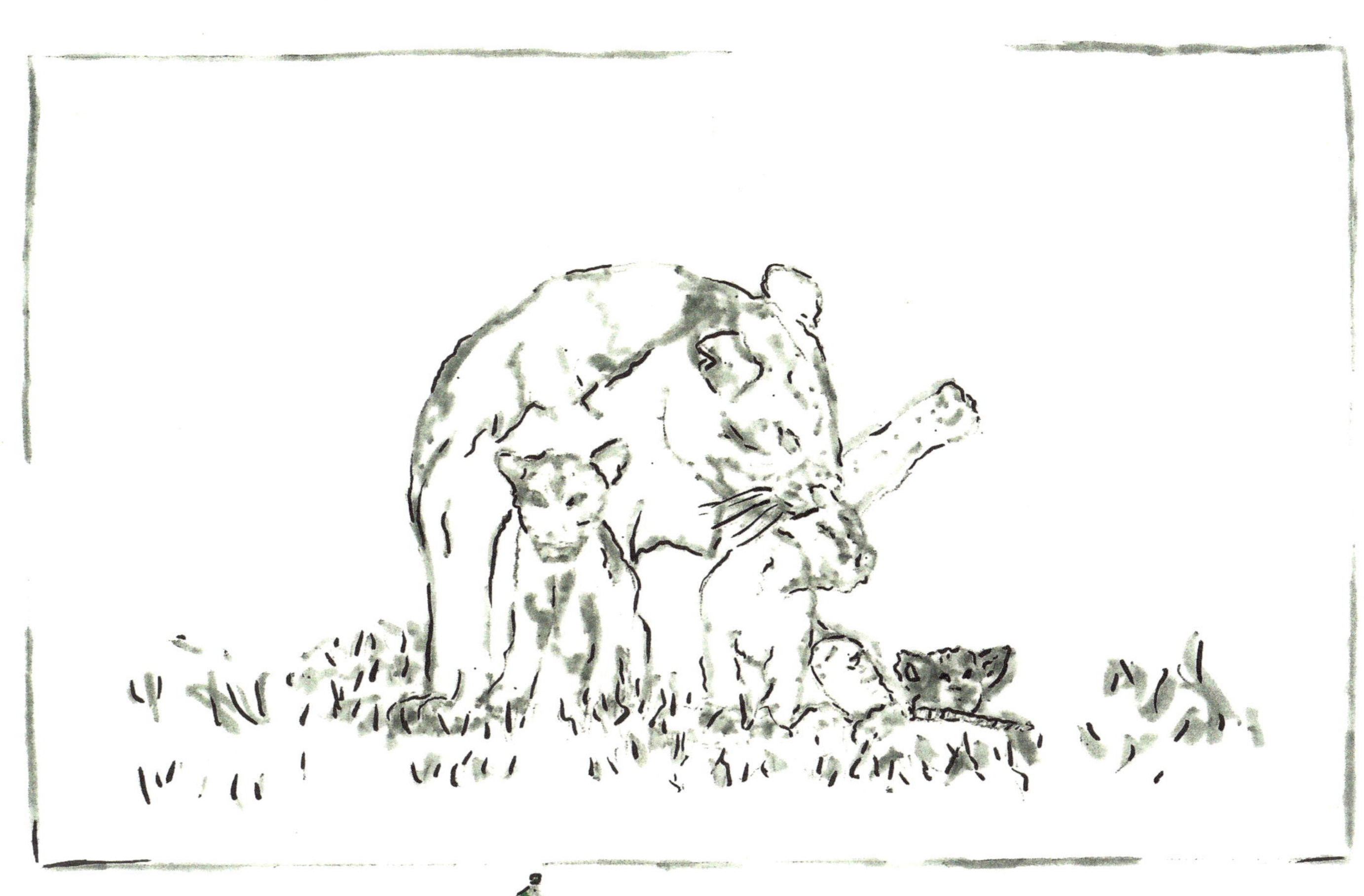

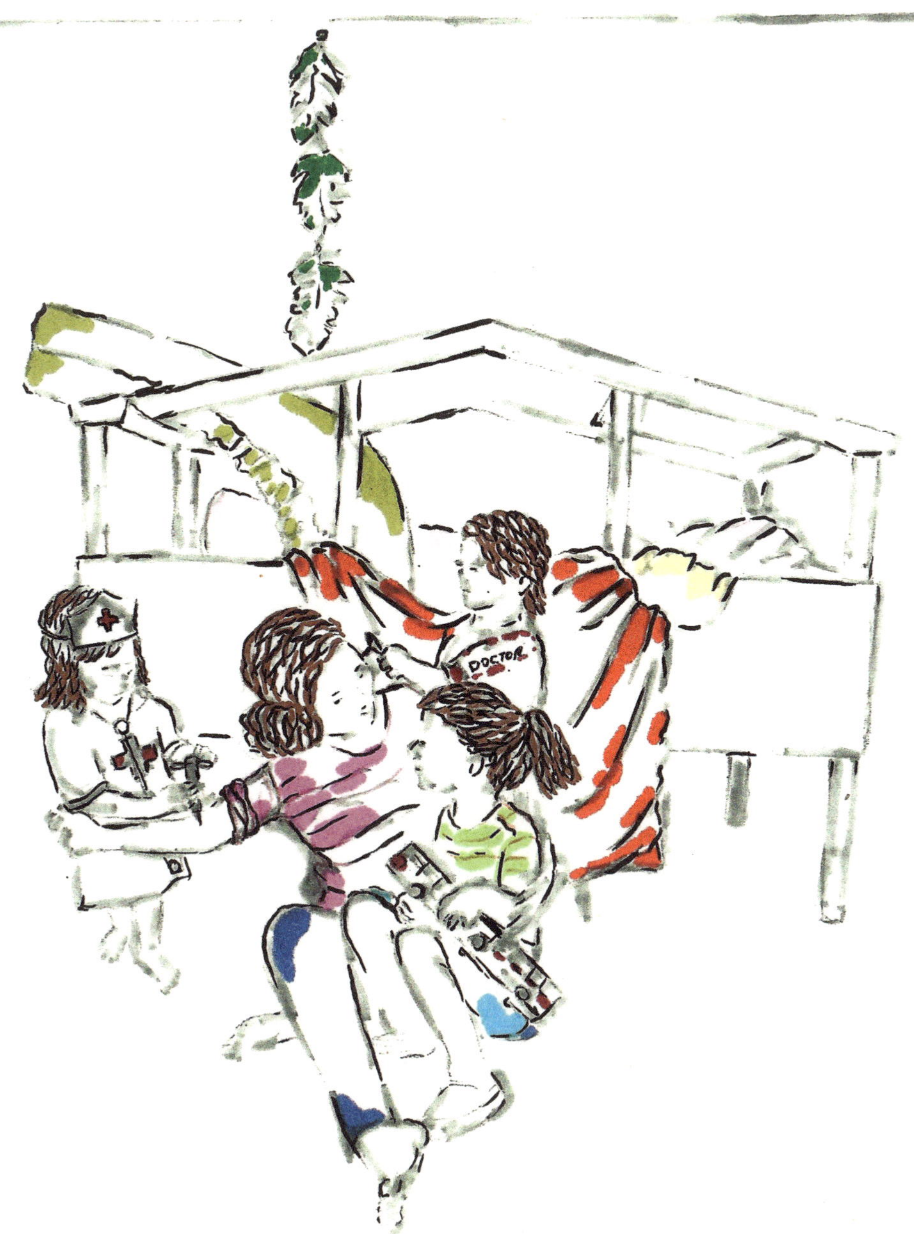
DOCTOR

Wann immer Jakob und Sophia Sehnsucht
nach ihrer Mama haben, holen sie die Fotoalben
hervor und erinnern sich mit Grossmutter
Assal an die schöne gemeinsame Zeit.
So finden sie Trost.

Whenever Jakob and Sophia miss their mama,
they get out the old photo albums with
Grandma Assal and remember the nice times
they had with Mama. That consoles them.

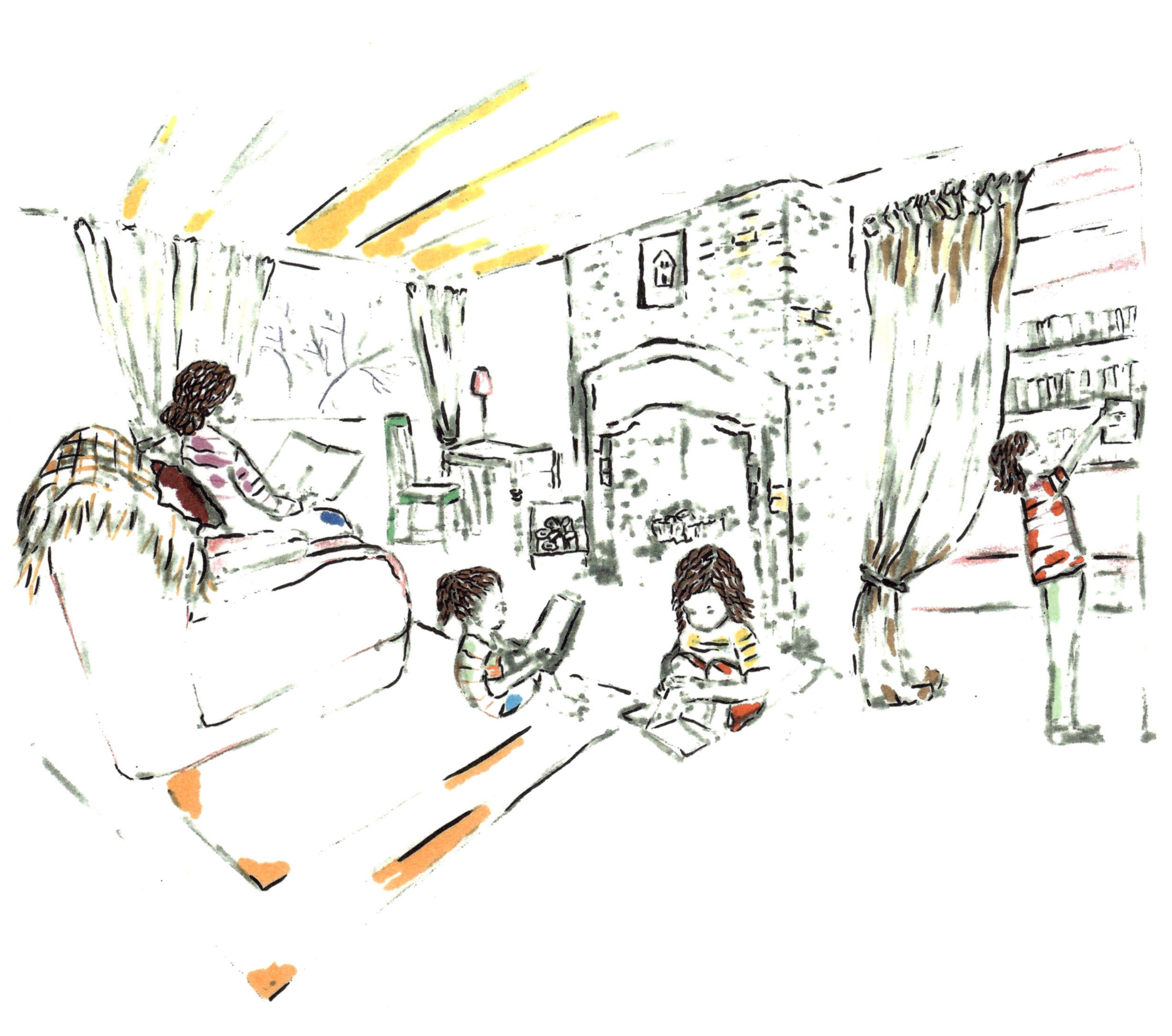

Nur der kleine Jonathan kann keinen Trost finden,
da er sich nicht mehr an seine Mutter erinnert.
Traurig schmiegt er sich in die Arme seiner
Oma: „Ich möchte mich auch an Mama erinnern!"
Jonathan muss bald ins Spital. Er muss operiert
werden, und davor hat er grosse Angst.

Only it doesn't console little Jonathan because
he can't remember his mother anymore. His
grandma cradles him in her arms. "I want to
remember my mama too!" he says sadly. Jonathan
has to go to the hospital soon, he's going to have
an operation and he's very frightened.

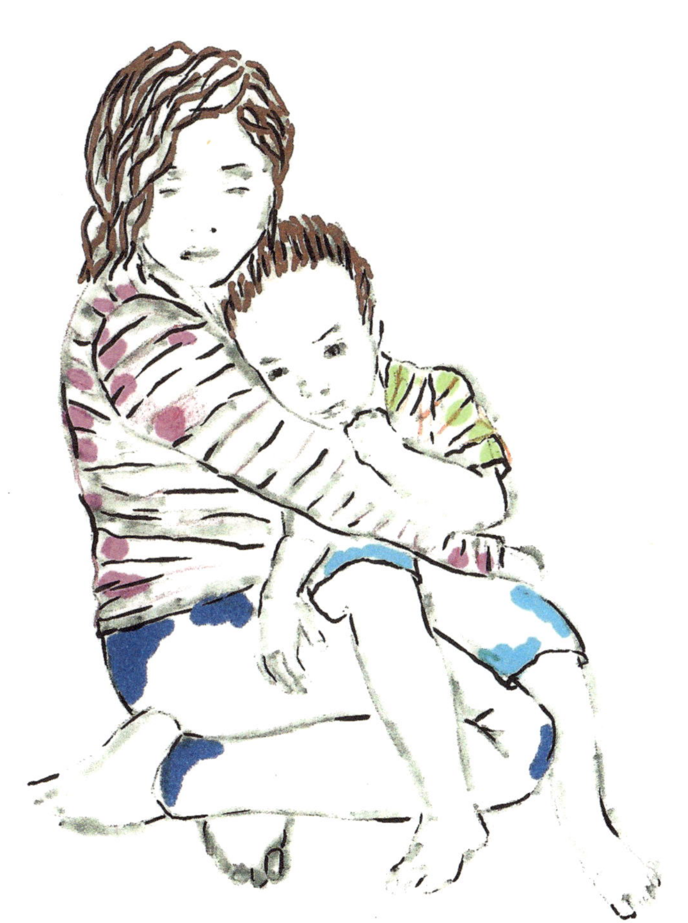

Am nächsten Tag, als sie alle am Tisch sitzen und Ostereier bemalen, sagt die Grossmutter: „Kinder, ich möchte euch jetzt ein Geheimnis verraten. Es gibt ein fliegendes Boot, das bis an die Schwelle zwischen dem Universum und der Ewigkeit segelt. Dort befindet sich eure Mutter. Jonathan, ich möchte, dass du mutig die Augen schliesst und fest daran glaubst, mit dem fliegenden Boot zu schweben. Du wirst deine Mama wiedersehen, und das wird dir Mut geben. Hab keine Angst, denn nach der Operation wirst du wieder gesund sein. Nach deiner Rückkehr wirst du furchtlos sein und die wunderschöne Welt erkunden.“

The next day, as they're all sitting around the table painting Easter eggs, Grandma says, "Children, I want to tell you a secret. There is a Flying Boat that sails all the way to the threshold between the Universe and the Everafter, which is where your mama is now. Jonathan, I want you to be brave, close your eyes and believe with all your heart that you're flying through the air on the Flying Boat. You'll see your mama again, and she'll give you courage. Don't be afraid, because after the operation you'll be right as rain again. When you get back you'll be dauntless and ready to go out and explore this beautiful world."

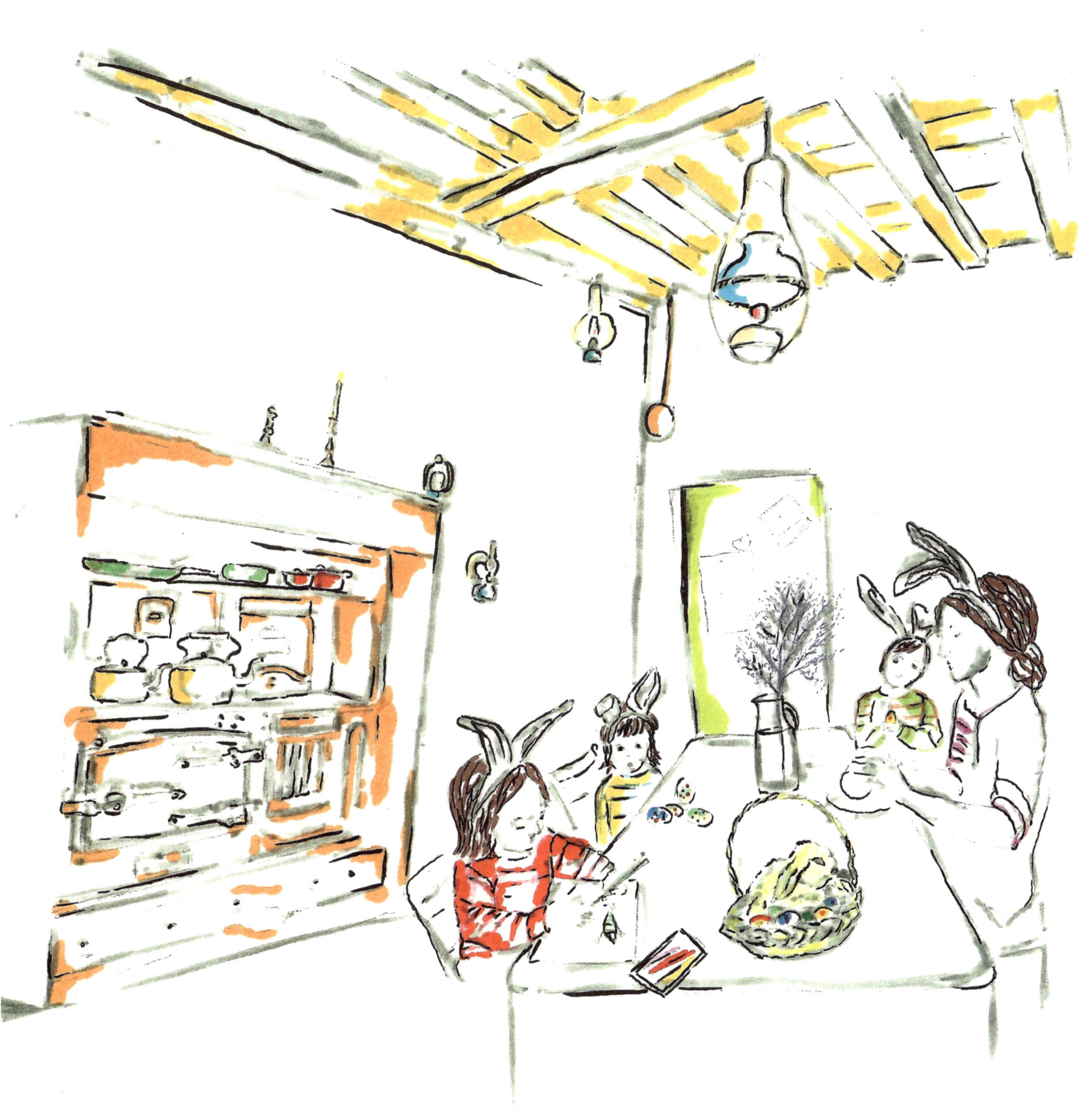

Es ist Vollmond, und alle machen sich zusammen
auf den Weg zum Strand, wo das fliegende Boot
auf sie wartet. Singend gehen sie durch den Wald.

It's a full moon, and they sing songs while making
their way through the forest to the beach, where
the Flying Boat awaits them.

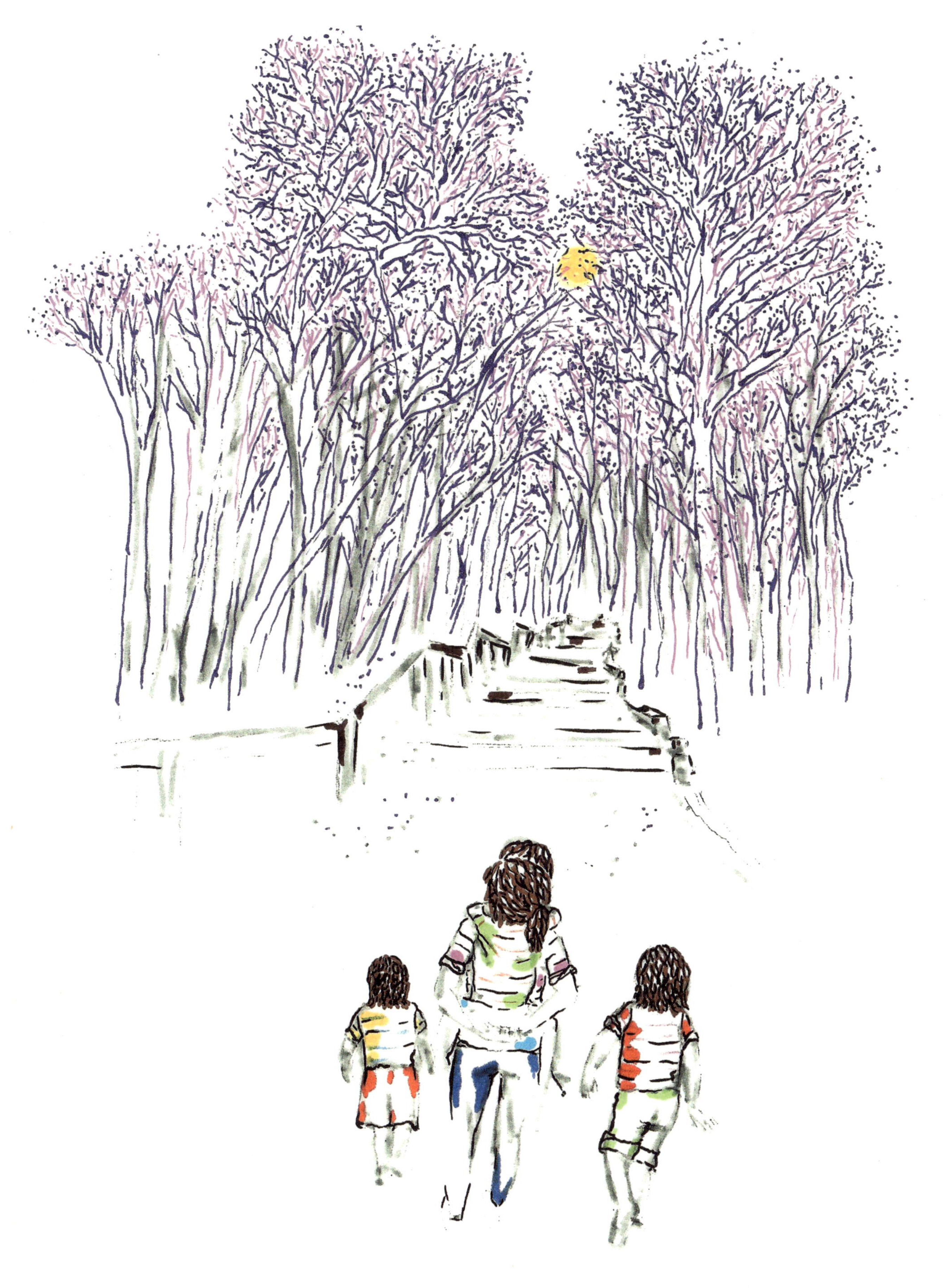

Als sie am Meeresufer ankommen, sehen sie
Delphine, die fröhlich aus den Wellen springen.

Reaching the shore, they see dolphins merrily
leaping out of the waves.

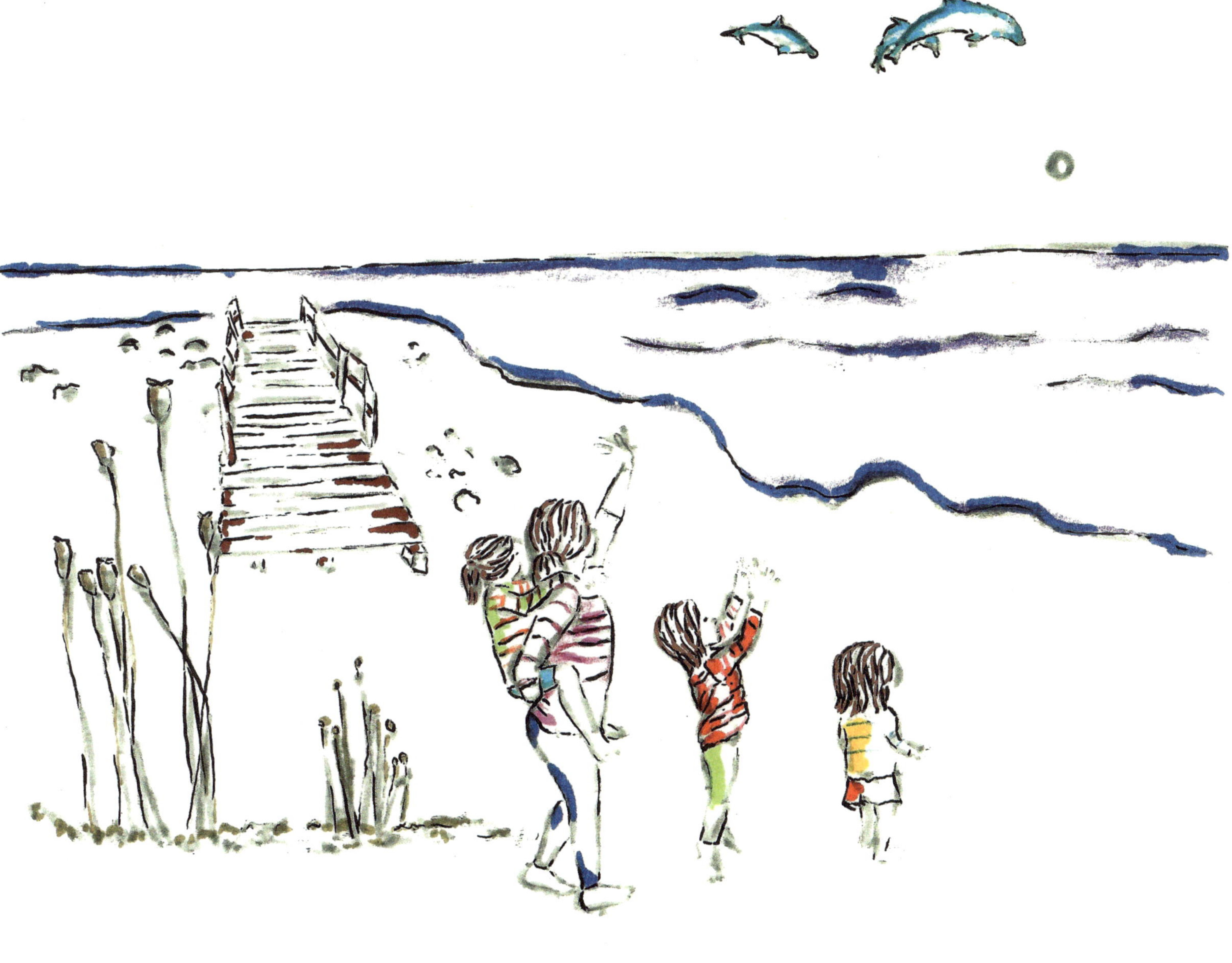

Plötzlich wird es ganz dunkel, und die Kinder
sehen das fliegende Boot im nebligen Nacht-
himmel auftauchen. „Es ist soweit", sagt die
Grossmutter.

Suddenly, it grows dark, and the Flying Boat
appears in the foggy night sky. "The time has
come," says Grandma.

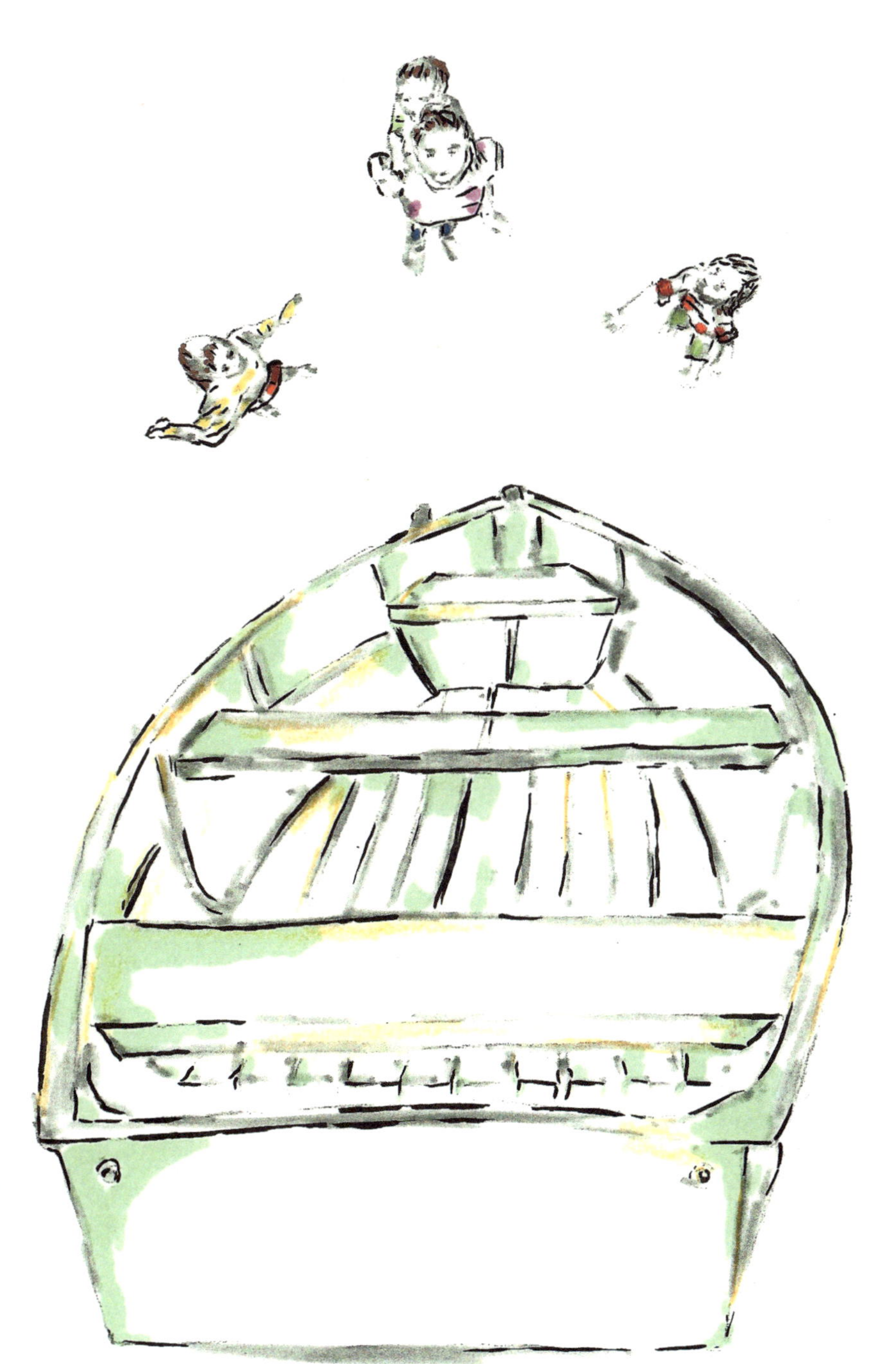

Jakob und Sophie schliessen mutig die Augen und glauben fest daran, mit dem fliegenden Boot zu segeln. Nur Jonathan hat Angst und zögert noch.

Als Jonathans Geschwister nach einer Weile die Augen wieder öffnen, erzählen sie aufgeregt von ihrer Reise und dem kostbaren Erlebnis, ihre Mama mit dem fliegenden Boot besucht zu haben. Und sie haben eine Botschaft für ihren kleinen Bruder: „Mama sagt, du sollst keine Angst vor der Operation haben! Schliess mutig die Augen und glaub fest daran, dass nach deiner Reise mit dem fliegenden Boot alles gut sein wird. Mama wartet auf dich, Jonathan!"

Plucking up their courage, Jakob and Sophie close their eyes and really believe they're soaring aloft on the Flying Boat. Only Jonathan is still afraid and hesitates.

After a while, Jakob and Sophie open their eyes again and excitedly recount their voyage on the Flying Boat and how wonderful it was to see Mama again. And they've brought back a message for their little brother: "Mama says not to be afraid of the operation! Now take heart, close your eyes and really believe everything will be all right after your voyage on the Flying Boat. Mama's waiting for you, Jonathan!"

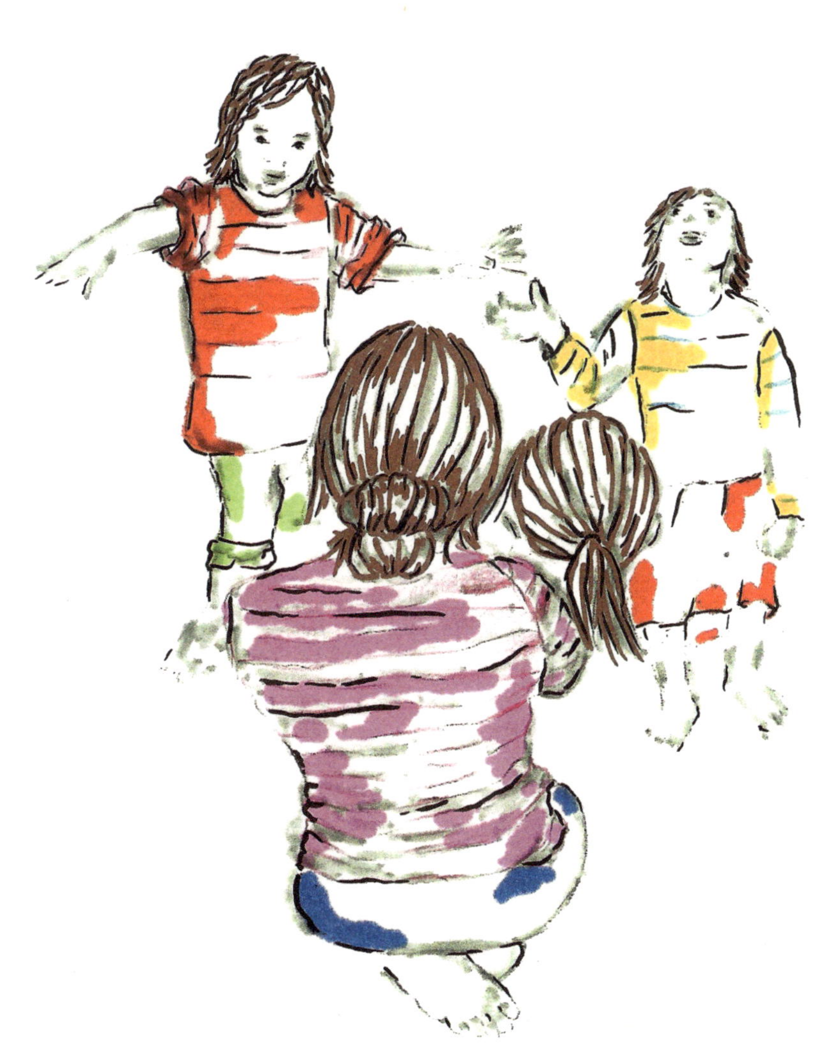

Jonathan nimmt seinen ganzen Mut zusammen,
und er spürt, wie seine Angst verfliegt.
Er schliesst die Augen und glaubt fest daran,
auf dem fliegenden Boot in den Himmel zu
schweben. Es funktioniert! Jonathan steigt mit
dem fliegenden Boot immer höher und höher
auf, bis zur Schwelle zwischen Universum und
Ewigkeit. Und plötzlich taucht seine Mama
auf, umhüllt von ihrer zart rosafarbenen Aura.
Sie ist wunderschön und strahlt Wärme und
Güte aus.

Jonathan gathers all his courage and feels his
fears evaporate. He shuts his eyes and really
believes he's floating up into the sky on the
Flying Boat. And it works! Jonathan soars higher
and higher on the Flying Boat, all the way up
to the threshold between the Universe and the
Everafter. And suddenly his mama appears
amid her soft pink aura. She is beautiful and
radiates warmth and kindness.

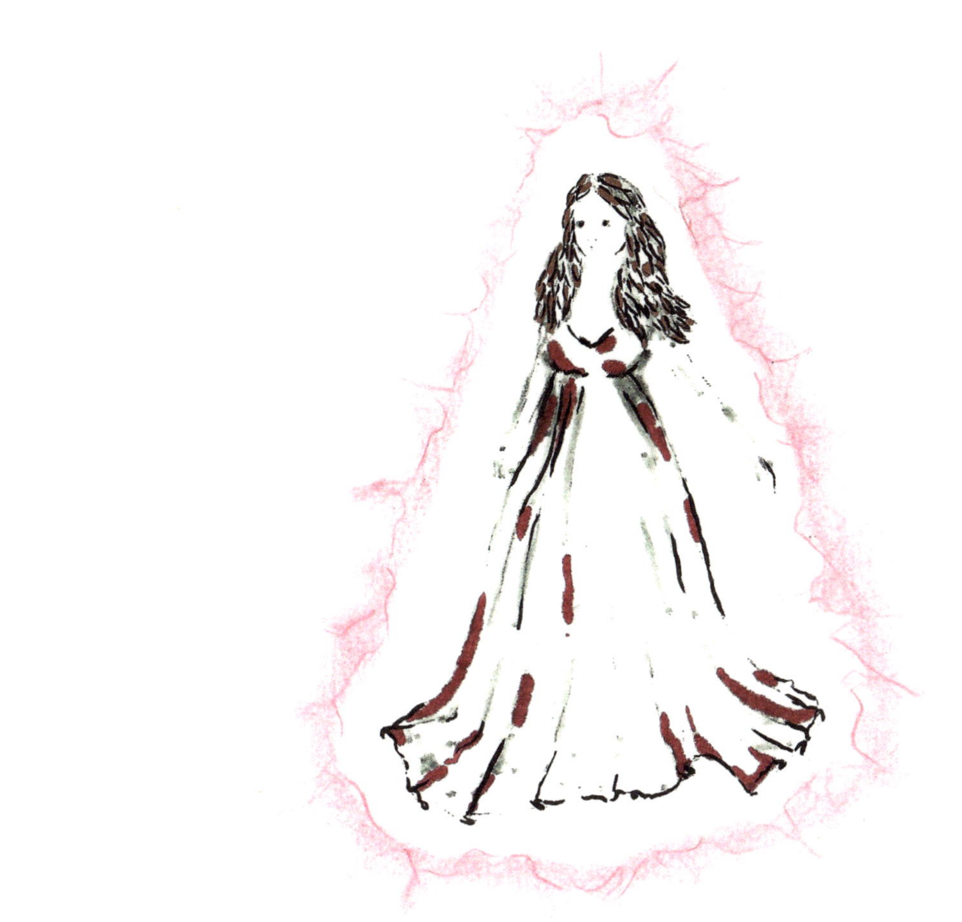
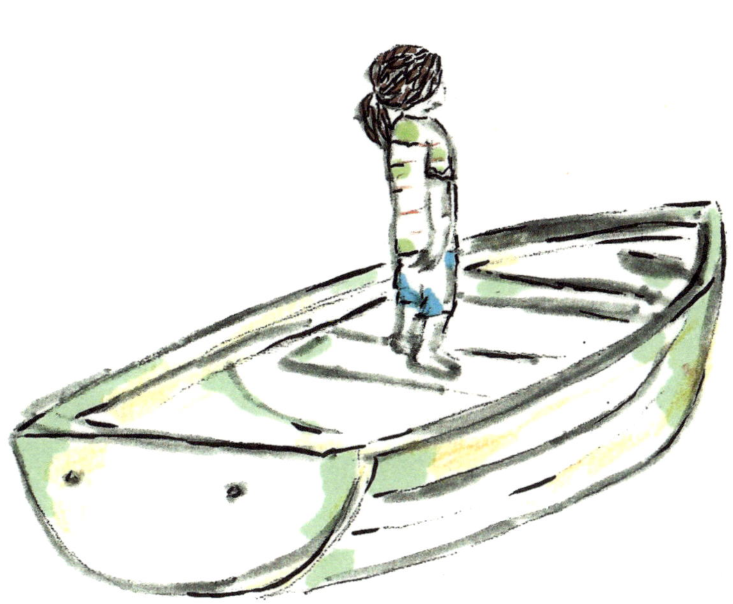

Sie breitet ihre Arme aus: „Komm her,
mein kleiner tapferer, mutiger Jonathan!"

She holds out her arms to her son: "Come
here, my brave, valiant little Jonathan!"

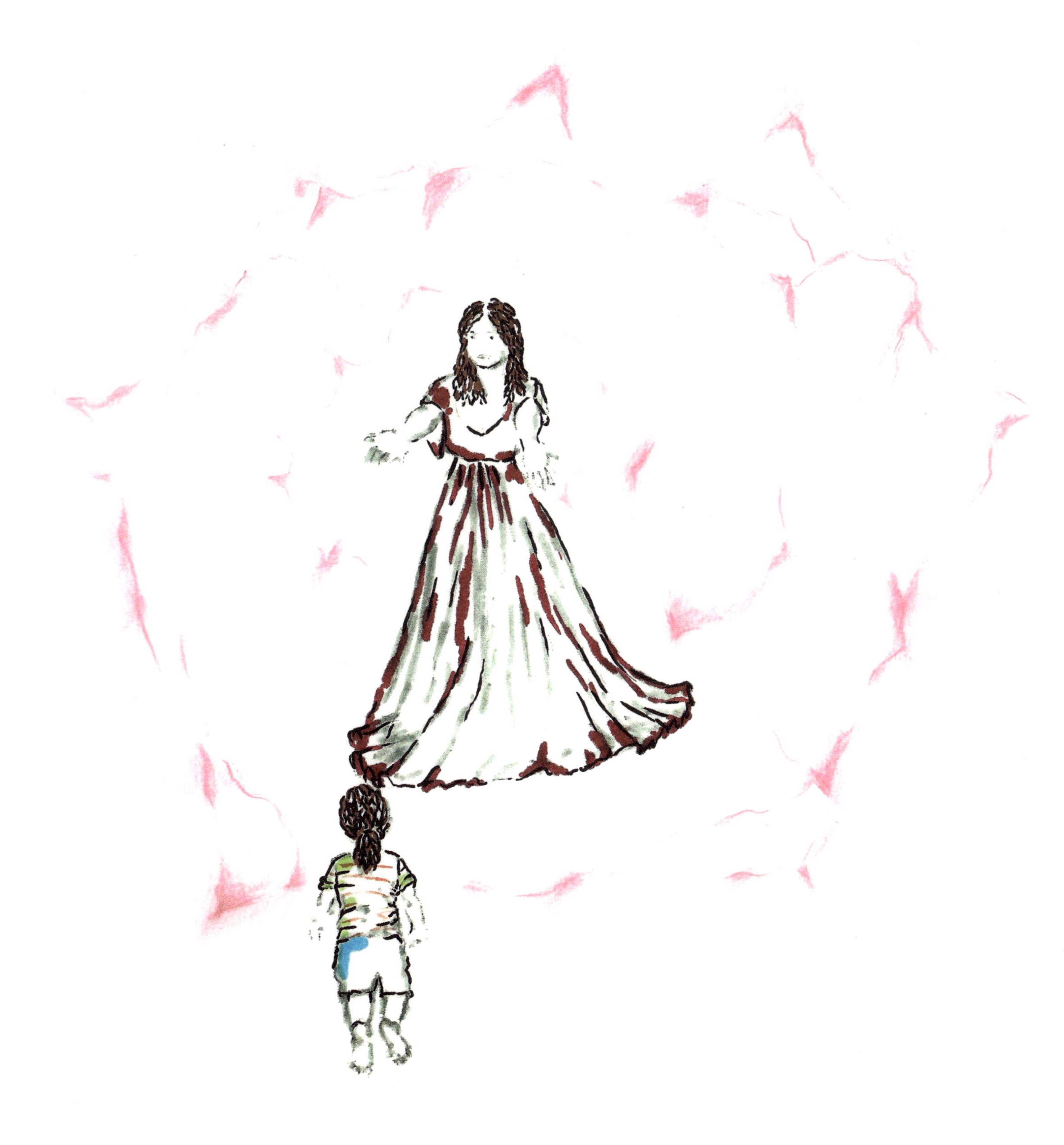

Sie umarmen sich ganz fest.

They hug and hold each other tight.

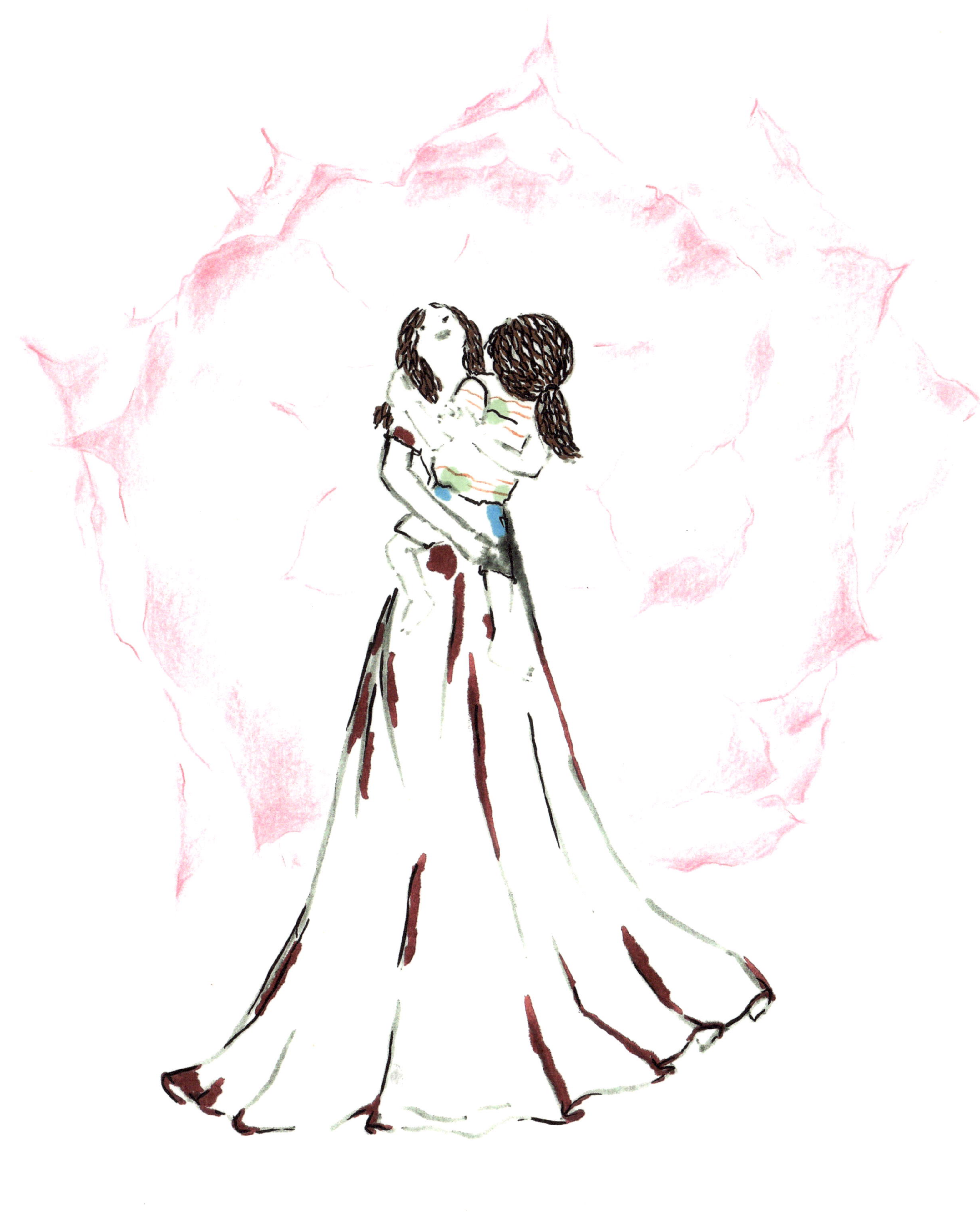

Jonathan erzählt seiner Mama von dem
Hund, seinen Freunden und von dem
Baumhaus, das er mit seinen Geschwistern
gebaut hat. Aufmerksam hört sie zu.
Jonathan könnte ihr die ganze Nacht von
seinen Erlebnissen erzählen.

Jonathan tells his mama about his dog, his
friends and the tree house he built with his
brother and sister. She listens attentively.
He could go on all night telling her about all
the things he's seen and done.

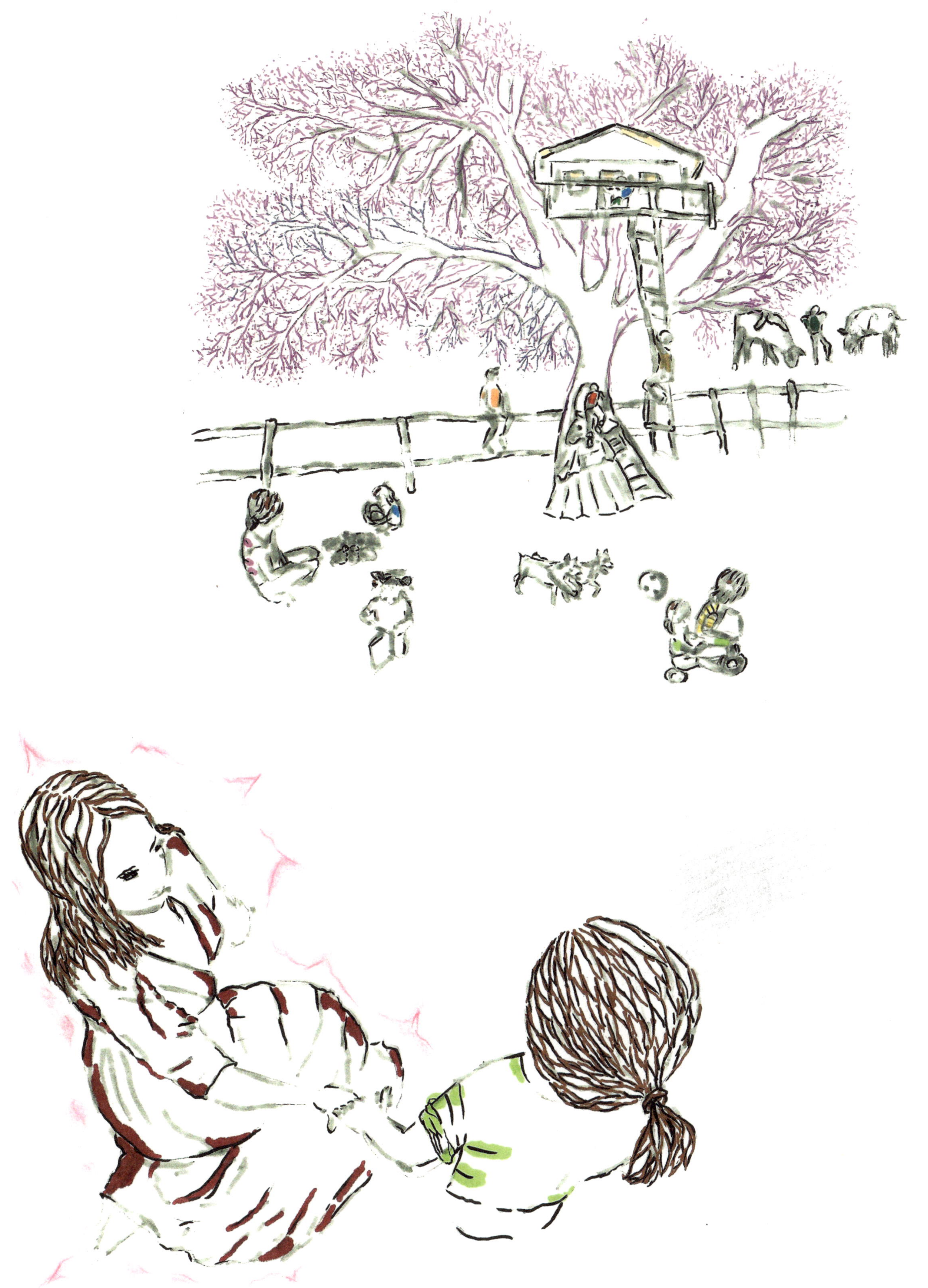

Nach einer Weile beginnt das fliegende Boot
sanft hin und her zu schaukeln. Die Zeit ist
gekommen, Abschied zu nehmen.

Louise nimmt Jonathan auf ihren Schoss:
„Wir werden uns wiedersehen. Bis dahin musst
du mir versprechen, ein glückliches Leben zu
führen." „Das verspreche ich dir!", antwortet
Jonathan.

Als er die Augen wieder öffnet, fühlt er sich
mutiger als je zuvor. Er ist sehr glücklich, da er
weiss, dass er nun den grössten Schatz besitzt:
die Erinnerung an seine Mutter bis in die
Ewigkeit.

After a while the Flying Boat begins to rock
gently back and forth. The time has come to
say goodbye.

Jonathan's mama sits him on her lap: "We shall
meet again. Until then, you must promise me
to lead a happy life." "I promise," says Jonathan.

When he opens his eyes again, he feels braver
than ever. And happier than ever because he
knows he now has the greatest treasure of all:
the memory of his mama for ever after.

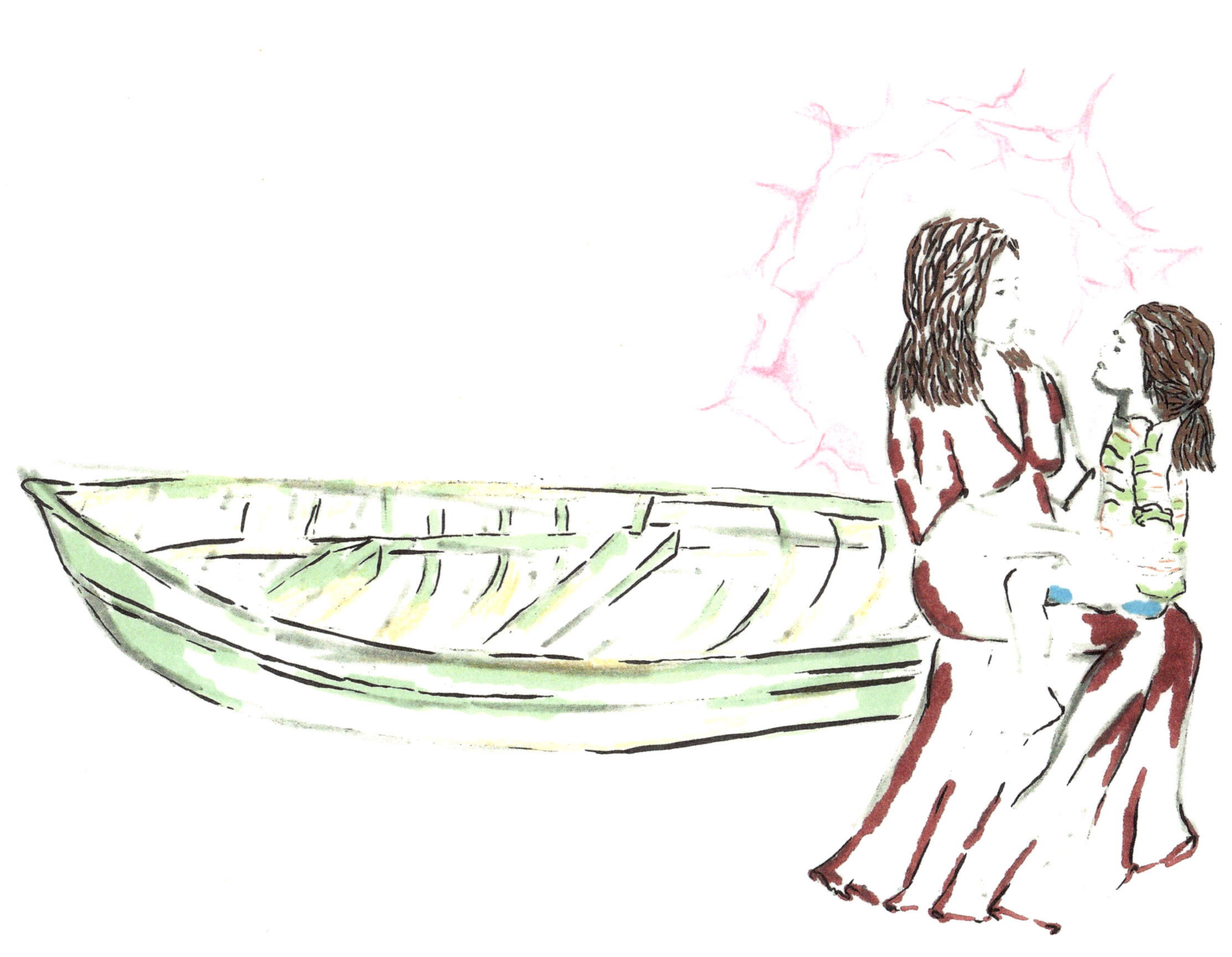

Brief an die geliebte Mama

A Letter to Dear Mom

Brief an die geliebte Mama

Liebste Mama, ich weiss jetzt, wie es sich anfühlt,
eine auf sich allein gestellte Soldatin zu sein, die
immer funktionieren muss, sich keine Krankheit
leisten kann und täglich ihre lange Pflichtenliste
abarbeiten muss.

Liebste Mama, ich weiss jetzt, wie es sich anfühlt,
wenn du auf dem Spielplatz all die perfekten Mütter
mit ihren perfekten Familien antriffst, die von jeder
Seite Hilfe bekommen und trotzdem unzufrieden
und überfordert sind. Und die dich dann fragen,
wie du das alles alleine von A bis Z bewältigst, dich
bemitleidend anschauen, um sich dann abzuwenden
und dich alleine stehen zu lassen, während in dir
Verletzungen und Enttäuschungen wieder hoch-
kommen und du dich traurig fühlst.

A Letter To Dear Mom

Dear Mom, now I know what it feels like to be a
soldier who's on her own and has to function all the
time, who can't afford to get sick and has to work
her way down a long to-do list every single day.

Dear Mom, now I know what it feels like to see all
the perfect mothers with their perfect families at
the playground, who get help from everyone and
yet still feel dissatisfied and overwhelmed. And
who then ask you how you cope with it all by
yourself, with a look of pity in their eyes, only to
turn away and leave you standing there all alone,
while hurts and disappointments well up inside
you and you feel sad.

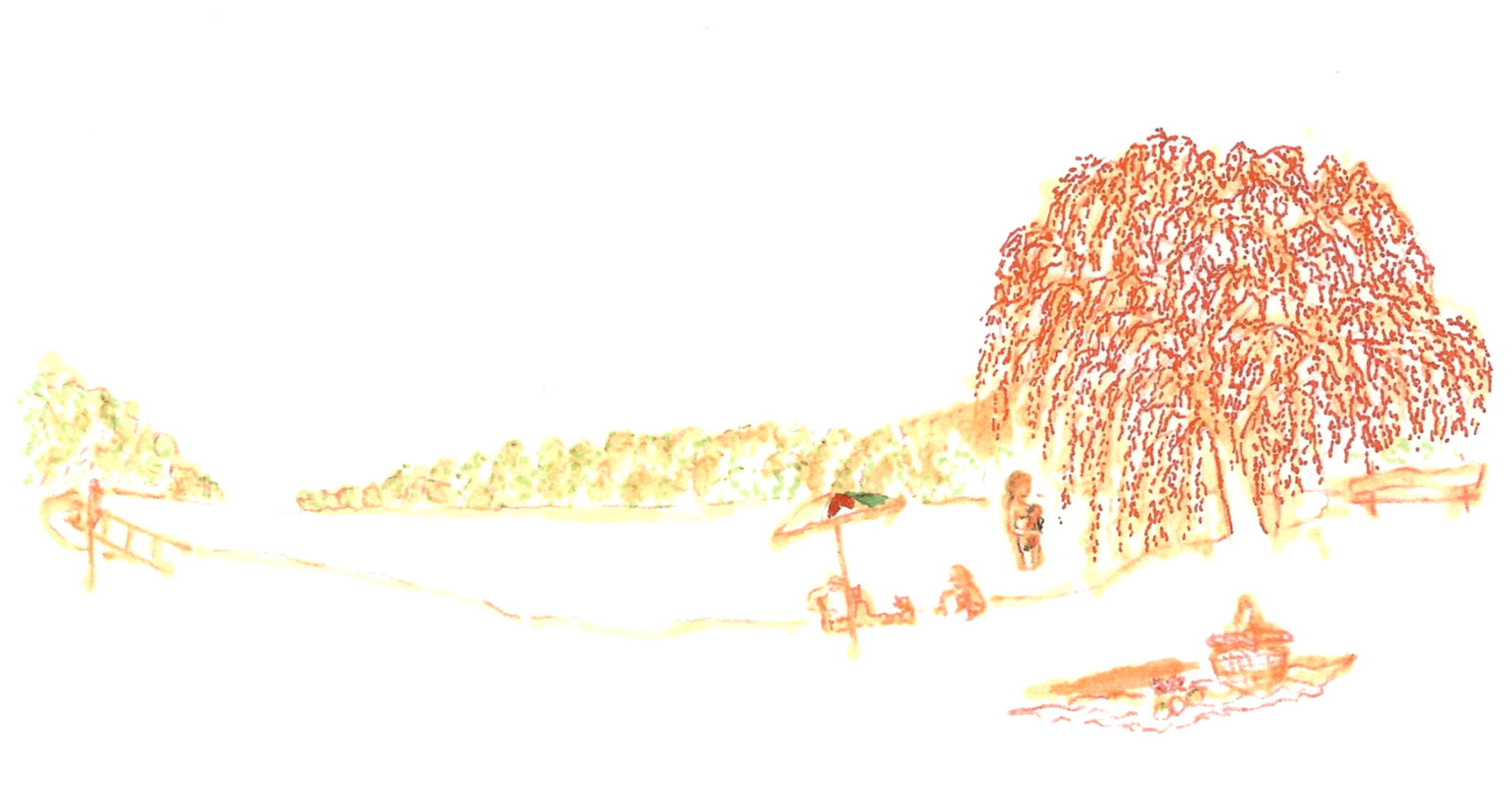

Liebste Mama, ich weiss jetzt, wie es ist, wenn die
neue Hausverwaltung, von Gier getrieben, ankün-
digt, die Miete verdoppeln zu wollen, und dir im
kalten Winter herzlos mit der Kündigung droht, und
wie Existenzängste dir die ganze Kraft rauben, die
du brauchst, um weiterhin eine Soldatin zu sein.

Liebste Mama, ich weiss jetzt, wie es ist, wenn du
die Wochenenden mit möglichst vielen Aktivitäten
gestaltest, damit dein Kind glücklich ist, du aber am
Sonnabend zu zweifeln beginnst, ob die von dir er-
schaffene Welt nicht doch irgendwann zusammen-
bricht. Ich weiss jetzt, wie es ist, sich als Versagerin
und schlechte Mutter zu fühlen, weil du deinem
Kind keine perfekte Familie bieten kannst, und dich
der Gedanke quält, dein Kind bräuchte mehr.

Liebste Mama, ich möchte dir damit sagen, dass es
gut ist, wenn dir manchmal alles zu viel wird und
du schreien und weinen musst. Es ist gut, wenn
manche Mütter, die dir begegnen, keinerlei Empathie
besitzen, da dir bewusst wird, wie stark du doch
bist und dass du Respekt verdienst. Es ist gut, wenn
dir wieder einmal seelenlose, gierige Menschen
Sorgen bereiten, da du immer wieder einen Weg
aus der Sackgasse findest, weil du gelernt, hast zu
kämpfen, und weil dein Leben wahrhaftig ist.

Liebste Mama, du stehst als Symbol für Wachstum,
Fürsorge, Tatkraft, Erkenntnis und emotionale Er-
fahrungen. Du stehst für das Prinzip von Werden,
Geben, Nehmen und Neubeginn. Du bist die Heldin
deiner fruchtbaren Landschaft. Ich bin dankbar,
dass ich durch dich die bedingungslose Liebe
erfahren habe.

Dear Mom, now I know what it's like when the greedy
new landlord announces plans to double the rent
and mercilessly threatens to throw you out on the
street in the cold winter, and how fears for your
livelihood rob you of all the strength you need to
soldier on.

Dear Mom, now I know what it's like when you pack
the weekends with as many activities as possible
to keep your kid happy, but on Saturday you're
already beginning to wonder whether this world
you've created isn't going to fall apart at some point.
Now I know what it's like to feel like a failure and
a bad mother because you can't offer your child a
perfect family and you're tormented by the thought
that your child needs more.

Dear Mom, what I mean to say is that it's a good
thing if sometimes it all becomes too much for you
and you have to scream and cry. It's a good thing
if some mothers you meet don't show any empathy,
because it drives home to you how strong you are
and that you deserve respect. It's a good thing when
greedy, soulless people cause you trouble, because
you always find a way out of the impasse, because
you've learned to fight, and because your life is
authentic.

Dear Mom, to me, you symbolize growth, care,
energy, insight and emotional experience. You
stand for the concepts of becoming, giving, taking
and starting anew. You are the heroine of your
fertile landscape. I am grateful for having
experienced unconditional love through you.

In *Stories of Little and Big Blossoms* geht
es um Themen wie Fremdsein, Toleranz,
Wertschätzung des Lebens oder Muttersein.
Shirin Azari ermutigt in ihren Geschichten
Mütter und Kinder zu einem positiven
Umgang mit diesen wichtigen Fragen.

Die Autorin verarbeitet in ihren Geschichten
ihre eigenen unsteten Kindheits- und Jugend-
jahre. Sie liess sich nicht unterkriegen, sondern
lernte schon früh, sich durchzukämpfen
und zu behaupten. Als Mutter eines Sohnes
erlebt sie immer wieder Situationen, die sie in
ihre Erzählungen einfliessen lässt.

Die Erlebnisse von Elham, Jonathan oder
Aylin, von der Autorin mit zarten, poetischen
Zeichnungen illustriert, sind eine eindringliche
Aufforderung zu Offenheit, Mut und Selbst-
bestimmung. Dabei sollen die Geschichten
die Aufmerksamkeit auf die unschuldigsten
aller Seelen lenken, auf die Kinder.

The *Stories of Little and Big Blossoms* are
about subjects like being a stranger in a
strange town, tolerance, treasuring life
and being a mom. Shirin Azari encourages
mothers and children to take a positive
approach to these formative experiences.

She processes her own unsettled childhood
and teenage years in her stories. Azari never
lost heart, but learned early in life to struggle
and assert herself. Now, as a mother raising
a son, she continually experiences situations
that she works into her stories.

The trials and tribulations of Elham, Jonathan
and Aylin, illustrated with Shirin Azari's
delicate, poetic drawings, are an insistent call
for openness, courage and self-determination.
The stories draw attention to the most
innocent souls of all, the children.

Shirin Azari (*1981, Bukan, Iran) ist eine iranische
Illustratorin, Autorin, Modedesignerin und
Schauspielerin. Am Lette-Verein, Berlin, studierte
sie Modedesign, anschliessend besuchte sie
die Film-Schauspielschule in Berlin sowie das
Lee Strasberg Institute in Los Angeles.
Seit 2002 arbeitet sie als Muse und Modell eng
mit dem Schweizer Fotografen Walter Pfeiffer
zusammen. Shirin Azari lebt und arbeitet in Berlin.

Shirin Azari (b. 1981 in Bukan, Iran) is a Berlin-
based Iranian illustrator, author, fashion designer
and actress. She studied fashion design at Berlin's
Lette-Verein and acting at the Film-Schauspielschule in Berlin and the Lee Strasberg Institute
in Los Angeles. Since 2002 she has been Swiss
photographer Walter Pfeiffer's muse and model.

Colophon

Shirin Azari: Stories of Little and Big Blossoms

Text & illustrations: Shirin Azari
Translation: Eric Rosencrantz
Proofreading: Miriam Wiesel, Eric Rosencrantz

Book design: Bogislav Ziemer
Printed and bound by DZA Druckerei zu Altenburg GmbH
Paper: Munken Print white 115g/qm
Cover: Peydur lissé 130 g/qm
Font: AdornS Slab Serif

First edition: Edition Patrick Frey, 2020
Print run: 700 copies
ISBN 978-3-906803-80-7
Printed in Germany

© 2020 drawings & texts: the author
© 2020 for this edition: Edition Patrick Frey

Edition Patrick Frey, Limmatstrasse 268, CH-8005 Zürich
www.editionpatrickfrey.com
mail@editionpatrickfrey.ch

Danksagung / Acknowledgments

An allererster Stelle danke ich Gott für meine Fügung.

Ich möchte mich bei Andrea Kempter für ihr Vertrauen in mein
Talent und die langjährige, herzliche und professionelle Künstler-
betreuung bedanken.

Mein herzlicher Dank geht an Patrick Frey und an das ganze Team
der Edition Patrick Frey, die mir die Möglichkeit gegeben haben,
mich als Autorin und Illustratorin zu verwirklichen. Meinem Mentor
Walter Pfeiffer und dem Grafiker Bogislav Ziemer danke ich für
ihre ständige Begleitung, Motivation und wahre Freundschaft.

Dieses Buch ist meiner grossen Inspiration gewidmet,
meinem Sohn Arian.

First and foremost, I thank God for my good fortune.

I would like to thank Andrea Kempter for believing in my talent
and for many years of warm and highly professional support.

My sincere thanks to Patrick Frey and the whole team at Edition
Patrick Frey, who gave me a chance to realize my potential as
a writer and illustrator. I thank my mentor Walter Pfeiffer and
graphic designer Bogislav Ziemer for their constant support,
encouragement and true friendship.

This book is dedicated to my great inspiration, my son Arian.

Distribution

Switzerland:
AVA Verlagsauslieferung, CH - Affoltern am Albis
ava.ch

Germany, Austria:
GVA Gemeinsame Verlagsauslieferung, D - Göttingen
gva-verlage.de

France, Luxembourg, Belgium:
Les presses du réel, F - Dijon
lespressesdureel.com

United Kingdom:
Antenne Books, GB - London
antennebooks.com

United States:
ARTBOOK / D.A.P., USA - New York
artbook.com

Japan:
twelvebooks, JP - Tokyo
twelve-books.com

Australia, New Zealand:
Perimeter Distribution, AU - Melbourne
perimeterdistribution.com

Rest of the world:
Edition Patrick Frey, CH - Zürich
editionpatrickfrey.com